CAMBRIDGE
UNIVERSITY PRESS

CAMBRIDGE PRIMARY
Global Perspectives

Learner's Skills Book 6

Adrian Ravenscroft & Thomas Holman

CAMBRIDGE
UNIVERSITY PRESS

University Printing House, Cambridge CB2 8BS, United Kingdom

One Liberty Plaza, 20th Floor, New York, NY 10006, USA

477 Williamstown Road, Port Melbourne, VIC 3207, Australia

314–321, 3rd Floor, Plot 3, Splendor Forum, Jasola District Centre, New Delhi – 110025, India

79 Anson Road, #06–04/06, Singapore 079906

Cambridge University Press is part of the University of Cambridge.

It furthers the University's mission by disseminating knowledge in the pursuit of education, learning and research at the highest international levels of excellence.

www.cambridge.org
Information on this title: www.cambridge.org/9781108926843

© Cambridge University Press 2021

First published 2021

20 19 18 17 16 15 14 13 12 11 10 9 8 7 6 5 4 3 2 1

Printed in India by Multivista Global Pvt Ltd.

A catalogue record for this publication is available from the British Library

ISBN 978-1-108-92684-3 Learner's Skills Book 6 Paperback with Digital Access (1 Year)

Cambridge University Press has no responsibility for the persistence or accuracy of URLs for external or third-party internet websites referred to in this publication, and does not guarantee that any content on such websites is, or will remain, accurate or appropriate. Information regarding prices, travel timetables, and other factual information given in this work is correct at the time of first printing but Cambridge University Press does not guarantee the accuracy of such information thereafter.

The learning objectives in this publication are reproduced from the Cambridge International Primary Global Perspectives curriculum framework. This Cambridge International copyright material is reproduced under licence and remains the intellectual property of Cambridge Assessment International Education.

Registered Cambridge International Schools benefit from high-quality programmes, assessments and a wide range of support so that teachers can effectively deliver Cambridge Primary. Visit www.cambridgeinternational.org/primary to find out more.

This text has not been through the Cambridge International endorsement process. Any references or material related to answers, grades, papers or examinations are based on the opinion of the authors.

....

Contents

Introduction

Welcome to Stage 6 of Cambridge Primary Global Perspectives.

What is this course all about? Well, Cambridge Global Perspectives™ is unique. The aim of the course is not a small one. The aim is for you to understand the world around you.

The world we live in is changing fast and the impacts of these global changes are felt right across the planet.

Learning in Cambridge Global Perspectives is about more than just understanding. It is about making a difference. That is why we have included examples of practical ways that you can try to make changes to your local area. You will learn about the global challenges we face, about issues such as sustainable transport and food supply. We will ask you to be to be innovative and engaged, and you will develop new skills in research and analysis, reflection and evaluation, collaboration and communication.

You will need to work in lots of different ways – on your own, in pairs and in groups – as you gain understanding of different perspectives and many crucial issues:

- How can you get even better at researching?
- How can you find out why people feel differently about an issue?
- How can you communicate your ideas to an audience – so that they understand the difference you want them to make?
- How can you judge the practical results of your actions?

These are big challenges, so this book provides regular opportunities for reflection and all the skills you need to succeed. Four characters (Zara, Marcus, Arun and Sofia) are with you every step of the way.

Each section follows a clear approach, guiding you through the stages of 'Starting with', 'Developing' and 'Getting better at' every skill, building your awareness of your progress and allowing you to take charge of your own learning journey. If you used our book for Stage 5, then you will recognise the structure of the lessons. Your challenge is to apply your skills in new ways, and in greater depth. Try to work independently sooner, and support your classmates who are less familiar with this way of working. A range of activities and tasks is included, with plenty of opportunities for peer-to-peer and group work, and to enable you to reflect on your progress, track your achievements and record your next steps. It contains a handy self-assessment at the end of each section so you can check your own progress as you gain essential understanding and new skills.

We hope you enjoy the challenges of this course and that you will have learnt how to make a positive contribution to a better future.

Adrian Ravenscroft and Tom Holman

How to use this book

This book contains lots of different features that will help your learning. These are explained below.

These are the learning objectives that will be covered in each lesson. ⟶

> **Research learning objectives**
>
> 1.1 Constructing research questions

You can use these learning goals to identify what you are learning in the lesson, and how you know when you have met your goals. ⟶

> **Lesson learning goals**
>
> These are the goals for this lesson.
> You will return to this table at the end of the lesson for the independent reflection activity.
>
> | My learning goals To start to: | I think | My teacher/ partner thinks |
> |---|---|---|
> | say what a global issue is | | |
> | identify different types of question | | |
> | make my own questions to help me understand global issues | | |

These are questions or tasks to help check what you already know before beginning a lesson. ⟶

> **Prior learning**
>
> What comes to mind when you think of 'global **issues**'?
>
> Have a class discussion.
>
> Take turns to say what you think the most important global issues are.

New and important words are orange in the text. You can find out what they mean in the glossary at the back of the book. ⟶

> Zara is thinking of questions that she could use for her topic.
> She has decided to work on: 'We need to do more recycling.'
> She has thought of many questions:

This helps you check how you are learning, and think about how well you are progressing with each goal at the end of each lesson. ⟶

Independent reflection activity

Check your learning goals

If you are sure you have met them and can give a reason why put '★'

If you think you have met them put '☺'

If you think you are not quite there yet put a '☺'

This allows you to consider your progress through the learning goals in a deeper way. The table encourages you to think about where you are on your learning journey, and give examples to show how you are progressing. You can choose goals to improve on in the future. ⟶

Self-assessment Lessons 1–2

How will I know if I have achieved my learning goals?

Use this activity to reflect on how well you have progressed over the last three lessons.

Tick (✓) 'Achieved' if you are sure you have made good progress with this skill and can give an example.

Tick (✓) 'Not there yet / with help' if you need some further practice so that you can make more progress.

If you tick 'Achieved', then challenge yourself to make further progress in the next section.

If you tick 'Not there yet / with help', there will be the chance to consolidate this skill in future lessons.

Communication learning objectives To start to:	Not there yet / with help	Achieved	Example
communicate information			
listen and respond			

This provides an opportunity to reflect on your Challenge topic as you progress through each skill. ⟶

Challenge topic review

Think about the Challenge topic you have been exploring and complete the following statements.

I was surprised to discover/explore that ....

....

I did not know ....

....

I now think ....

....

Register to access free supporting resources through Cambridge GO – the home for all of your Cambridge digital content. Visit cambridge.org/go

Acknowledgements

The authors and publishers acknowledge the following sources of copyright material and are grateful for the permissions granted. While every effort has been made, it has not always been possible to identify the sources of all the material used, or to trace all copyright holders. If any omissions are brought to our notice, we will be happy to include the appropriate acknowledgements on reprinting.

Thanks to the following for permission to reproduce images:

Cover by Omar Aranda (Beehive Illustration)

Unit 1 ChristianChan/GI; peeterv/GI; Sasirin Pamai/GI; lvcandy/GI; stellalevi/GI; Rosemary Calvert/GI; SOMPOP SRINOPHAN/GI; Xinzheng/GI; monkeybusinessimages/GI; homegrowngraphics/GI; Mint Images/GI; Klaus Vedfelt/GI; olaser/GI; Rosmarie Wirz/GI; Rapeepong Puttakumwong/GI; thianchai sitthikongsak/GI; xavierarnau/GI; mixetto/GI; Jake Wyman/GI; mrPliskin/GI; Yasser Chalid/GI; Marilyn Nieves/GI; Matthias Kulka/GI; Images By Tang Ming Tung/GI; SDI Productions/GI; Kittkavin Kao Ien/GI; Lalocracio/GI; Predrag Vuckovic/GI; Annika Gültzow/GI; Unit 2 Jenny Dettrick/GI; David Malan/GI; Deepblue4you/GI; Nadeem Khawar/GI; querbeet/GI; Yagi Studio/GI; TravelCouples/GI; John M Lund Photography Inc/GI; Yogendra Kumar/Hindustan Times/GI; Jose Luis Pelaez Inc/GI; bubaone/GI; Alexander Spatari/GI; Mehedi Hasan/NurPhoto/GI; SIMON MAINA/AFP/GI; Ablozhka/GI; ISerg/GI; sarayut Thaneerat/GI; ferrantraite/GI; Unit 3 Andrew Aitchison/In pictures/GI; Carol Yepes/GI; Atlantide Phototravel/GI; Alistair Berg/GI; Jamie Grill Photography/GI; BSIP/Universal Images Group/GI; Alistair Berg/GI; Jacobs Stock Photography Ltd/GI; Andrew Fox/GI; AIZAR RALDES/AFP/GI; Unit 4 doble-d/GI; Jens Kuhfs/GI; Kevin Summers/GI; Foodcollection RF/GI; Klaus Vedfelt/GI; Compassionate Eye Foundation/Chris Ryan/GI; Jamie Grill/GI; Mlenny/GI; Mehedi Hasan/NurPhoto/GI; Kevin Horgan/GI; FatCamera/GI; Thanasis Zovoilis/GI; Hill Street Studios/GI; Flashpop/GI; SDI Productions/GI; David Madison/GI; Hill Street Studios/GI; Thomas Barwick/GI; epicurean/GI; Westend61/GI; Unit 5 Rawpixel/GI; SolStock/GI; Marc Dufresne/GI; SolStock/GI; JamesBrey/GI; Thomas Barwick/GI; Hill Street Studios/GI; Klaus Vedfelt/GI; plusphoto/a.collectionRF/GI; Martin Barraud/GI; DaniloAndjus/GI; Unit 6 Francesco Carta fotografo/GI; ewg3D/GI; Orbon Alija/GI; Creative_Stock/GI; YE AUNG THU/AFP/GI; imtmphoto/GI; Thomas Barwick/GI; Klaus Vedfelt/GI; LumiNola/GI.

Key: GI= Getty Images.

1

Starting with research skills: Lesson 1

Research learning objectives

1.1 Constructing research questions

Lesson learning goals
These are the goals for this lesson. You will return to this table at the end of the lesson for the independent reflection activity.

My learning goals To start to:	I think	My teacher/ partner thinks
say what a global issue is		
identify different types of question		
make my own questions to help me understand global issues		

Prior learning
What comes to mind when you think of 'global issues'? Have a class discussion. Take turns to say what you think the most important global issues are.

Starter activity

Marcus is thinking of a global issue that matters in his home area.

Issue	Transport
Problems	• The school bus is not always on time and we become late. • The traffic is really bad when it is time to go to school. • Trucks in my area make really bad fumes.

Now think of a global issue that matters in your home area.

Write down the name of the issue and some of the problems it causes.

Issue	
Problems	• • • • • •

Main activity part 1

The topic I am working on today is:

....

Zara is thinking of questions that she could use for her topic.
She has decided to work on: 'We need to do more recycling.'
She has thought of many questions:

What gets thrown away in our school?

What resources is our world running out of?

What does the law say?

Where is the nearest recycling place?

What problems does waste cause in our area?

We need to do more recycling

What can we recycle in our country?

What problems does waste cause our planet?

What is the best way people can cut down on waste?

How can the government help?

Class discussion

What other questions could Zara add to her list?

Main activity part 2

Zara's group has thought of some good questions:

- some are about what happens in her area
- some are about what happens in her country
- some are about what happens all around the world.

Which is which? The first three have been done for you.

	Local question	National question	Global question
What gets thrown away in our school?	✓		
What does the law say?		✓	
What problems does waste cause our planet?			✓
Where is the nearest recycling place?			
What can be recycled in our country?			
How can the government help?			
What is the best way people can cut down on waste?			
What problems does waste cause in our area?			
What resources is our world running out of?			

Now with your group, think of questions that you could use for your topic.

Check you have thought of a good range of questions:

- some about what happens in your area
- some about what happens in your country
- some about what happens all around the world.

Use the template the teacher will give you to write your questions.

Share your ideas with others in the class.

Independent reflection activity

Check your learning goals

If you are sure you have met them and can give a reason why put a '★'.

If you think you have met them put a '☺'.

If you think you are not quite there yet put a '☺'.

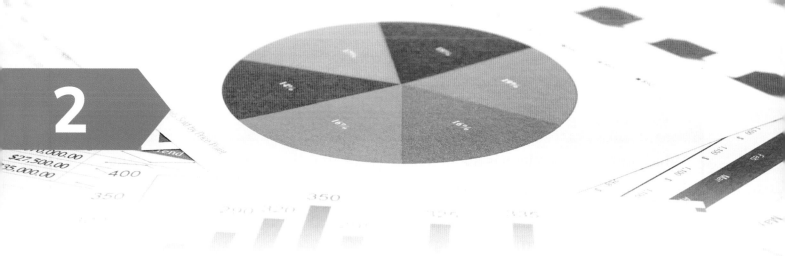

2

Starting with research skills: Lesson 2

Research learning objectives

1.2 Information skills

1.3 Conducting research

1.4 Recording findings

Lesson learning goals		
These are the goals for this lesson. You will return to this table at the end of the lesson for the independent reflection activity.		
My learning goals To start to:	I think	My teacher/ partner thinks
recognise different sources that can help me to find out about a topic		
design a questionnaire to use in an investigation		
make simple predictions about what I think I will find out in an investigation		
choose a suitable way of selecting, organising and recording what I find out		

Prior learning

Which of these questions is about a local issue, which is about a national issue and which is about a global issue?

Question	Local, national or global
1 What is the government doing to protect rare animals in our country?	
2 Which countries are doing most to prevent climate change?	
3 How can our school persuade learners to recycle more?	

Starter activity

Sofia and Marcus are deciding on a topic to investigate. They have thought of three questions. Where could they find information about each question?

1   What did people who are old now learn when they were at school?

They could find out about this by ....

2   What transport is the most popular way for learners to travel to our school?

They could find out about this by ....

3   What is the average size of classes in schools in different countries?

They could find out about this by ....

Now share your ideas with a partner. Decide the most useful source of information for each question and write it below.

1   What did people who are old now learn when they were at school?

The best way to find out would be ....

2   What transport is the most popular way for learners to travel to our school?

The best way to find out would be ....

3   What is the average size of classes in schools in different countries?

The best way to find out would be ....

Class discussion

1   What are some of the best ways of finding the answer to a local question?
2   How is finding the answer to a local question different to finding the answer to a national or global question?

Main activity part 1

The topic I am working on today is:

....

Sofia and Marcus investigated the topic 'What is the most popular way for learners to travel to school?' They asked other learners at their school about it.

This is how they recorded the other learners' answers:

HOW DO YOU TRAVEL TO SCHOOL?

Ahmed comes by bus

3 boys and 2 girls take the train

I use my bike when it's sunny

Jan and Hanna walk with their mum

on foot = 4

taxi ЖЖ

Ken and his friends travel in his dad's car

+ Usain

Class discussion

1 Is this the best way to record the information? Give some reasons for your answer.

2 What other method could the learner use to collect and organise the information?

Zara and Arun suggest collecting and recording information like this:

Investigation: What is the most popular way for learners to travel to our school?

Question we will ask: How do you travel to school?

Transport	Tally	Total
Car	IIII	4
Taxi	IIII	5
Bus	II	2
Train	IIII	5
Bicycle	I	1
Walk	II	2
Other		

3 What are the advantages of collecting and recording information like this?

Main activity part 2

Think of a similar type of question that you and a partner could ask your classmates.

Write your question in the template your teacher gives you to make your own questionnaire.

Now think of some of the different answers people could give to your question. Write these in the left column.

When you thought of the answers that people might give, you made a **prediction**. You thought about something that was likely to happen.

Now make another prediction. What do you think the most common answer to your question will be? Why do you think this?

My prediction: ....

Why I think this: ....

Peer feedback

Show your questionnaire to a partner, and ask them to tell you...

Two things that they like about it (write what they tell you here):

⭐ ....

⭐ ....

One thing that you could do better (write what they tell you here):

🌠 ....

Independent reflection activity

Check your learning goals

If you are sure you have met them and can give a reason why put a '★'.

If you think you have met them put a '☺'.

If you think you are not quite there yet put a '☺'.

3

Starting with research skills: Lesson 3

Research learning objectives

1.2 Information skills

1.3 Conducting research

1.4 Recording findings

<table>
<tr><td colspan="3">Lesson learning goals</td></tr>
<tr><td colspan="3">These are the goals for this lesson.
You will return to this table at the end of the lesson for the independent reflection activity.</td></tr>
<tr><td>My learning goals
To start to:</td><td>I think</td><td>My teacher/
partner thinks</td></tr>
<tr><td>find information in sources to answer my own questions</td><td></td><td></td></tr>
<tr><td>think of my own questions to ask when interviewing someone</td><td></td><td></td></tr>
<tr><td>recognise different ways of selecting, organising and recording information from sources</td><td></td><td></td></tr>
</table>

Prior learning

Make a prediction about:

- the weather tomorrow
- your first job
- the next world record to be broken.

Talk to a partner. What is a prediction?

Share your predictions with your partner. Which of your predictions are the same and which are different? Why?

Starter activity

At Zara and Arun's school, learners are often late in the morning. They want to investigate why this happens. What do you think?

Class discussion

1 Why are learners sometimes late to school in the morning?
2 What sources could you use to investigate this question?
3 What questions could you ask?
4 How could you record the results?

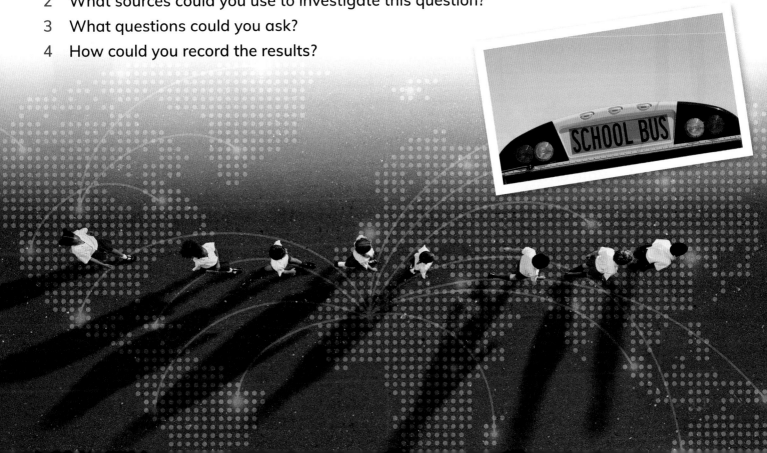

Main activity

The topic I am working on today is:

....

Zara and Arun have designed a questionnaire for their investigation:

Questionnaire: Travelling to school						
1 Type of transport	Car	Bus	Train	Bicycle	Walk	Other
2 Time taken	Less than 15 mins		15–30 mins		More than 30 mins	
3 People you travel with	By yourself		With other children		With adults	
4 Late arrival	Never late		Sometimes late		Often late	
5 Reason for late arrival						

Zara and Arun are going to interview other learners and record their answers on the questionnaire.

What questions will they ask? Write the questions here:

1 .... ?

2 .... ?

3 .... ?

4 .... ?

5 .... ?

Now interview a partner using your questions. Record their answers on the questionnaire.

Share your findings with the class.

Independent reflection activity

Check your learning goals

If you are sure you have met them and can give a reason why put a '★'.

If you think you have met them put a '☺'.

If you think you are not quite there yet put a '☺'.

Self-assessment Lessons 1–3

How will I know if I have achieved my learning goals?

Use this activity to reflect on how well you have progressed over the last three lessons.

Tick (✓) 'Achieved' if you are sure you have made good progress with this skill and can give an example.

Tick (✓) 'Not there yet / with help' if you need some further practice so that you can make more progress.

If you tick 'Achieved', then challenge yourself to make further progress in the next section.

If you tick 'Not there yet / with help', there will be the chance to **consolidate** this skill in future lessons.

Continued

Research learning objectives To start to:	Not there yet / with help	Achieved	Example
construct research questions			
use information skills			
conduct research			
record findings			

Reflect on your responses in your self-assessment and identify one area for improvement.

One area I want to improve in is:

....

How I will improve:

....

Challenge topic review

Think about the Challenge topic you have been exploring and complete the following statements.

I was surprised to discover/explore that ....

....

I did not know ....

....

I now think ....

....

Developing research skills: Lesson 4

Research learning objectives

1.1 Constructing research questions

1.2 Information skills

Lesson learning goals		
These are the goals for this lesson. You will return to this table at the end of the lesson for the independent reflection activity.		
My learning goals To develop my knowledge and understanding about:	I think	My teacher/ partner thinks
making questions that help me investigate a topic		
deciding what sources will help me find out more about a topic		

Prior learning

Sort these ideas into two groups in the table below:

- interviewing people
- making a graph or chart
- making a prediction
- making a table

- making a **tally** chart
- reading articles online
- taking notes
- using a questionnaire.

Ways of carrying research	Ways of recording results

Check your results with a partner to see if you agree.

Starter activity

At Sofia and Marcus's school, there is a problem with litter on the playground. Sofia and Marcus have different **perspectives** on why this happens. Read what they say about the problem:

I do not agree. The problem is there is only one **bin**. When it gets full, there is nowhere to put your litter.

Kids round here do not care. They see so much litter they think it is normal.

Class discussion

Whose perspective do you share most? Marcus's or Sophia's? Why?

Main activity

The topic I am working on today is:

....

Zara and Arun have been listening to Marcus and Sofia's discussion. They would like to find out more so that they can decide whose perspective they agree with.

1 What sources would help them decide if they agree with Marcus or Sofia? Number these sources from 1 (most helpful) to 6 (least helpful).

- Articles in the local newspaper $\square$

- Documentaries on local TV $\square$

- Other children at their school $\square$

- Teachers and parents of children at their school $\square$

- Textbooks in the school library $\square$

- The school's website and blog $\square$

2 What questions could they ask?

....

....

....

....

....

Class discussion

1   Which source do you think would be most helpful to Zara and Arun? Why?

2   Who would be most useful for Zara and Arun to talk to? Why?

3   What other actions could they take to get a full understanding of the problem?

Independent reflection activity
Check your learning goals
If you are sure you have met them and can give a reason why put a '★'.
If you think you have met them put a '☺'.
If you think you are not quite there yet put a '☹'.

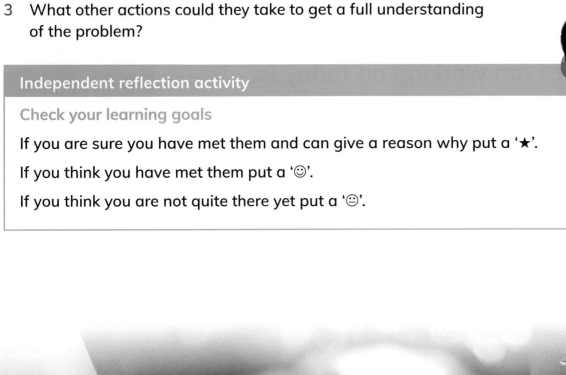

5

Developing research skills: Lesson 5

Research learning objectives

1.2 Information skills

1.3 Conducting research

1.4 Recording findings

Lesson learning goals		
These are the goals for this lesson. You will return to this table at the end of the lesson for the independent reflection activity.		
My learning goals To develop my knowledge and understanding about:	I think	My teacher/ partner thinks
reading a tally chart		
using the results of a questionnaire		
looking at results and using them to suggest a course of action		

Prior learning

1 In Lesson 4, what was the issue that Sofia and Marcus were trying to resolve?
2 What was Sofia's perspective?
3 What was Marcus's perspective?
4 Who did you agree with most? What were your reasons for thinking this?

Starter activity

After they talked to 20 children at their school, these are the results obtained by Sofia and Marcus.

There is too much litter on the school playground at break time.

Strongly agree	Agree	Do not know	Disagree	Strongly disagree
HHH HHH II	HHH II		I	

Children drop litter because they do not care about the environment.

Strongly agree	Agree	Do not know	Disagree	Strongly disagree
	II	I	HHH HHH	HHH II

There are not enough litter bins on the playground for everyone's rubbish.

Strongly agree	Agree	Do not know	Disagree	Strongly disagree
HHH HHH HHH I	III		I	

What do we know for sure from the information? Can we draw any conclusions from this evidence? Make notes ready for the class discussion.

Class discussion

What do we know for sure from these results?

Main activity

The topic I am working on today is:

Sofia and Marcus looked at their results and talked about what it might all mean.

It is time to do something about all this litter now!

Yes, but we need to be clear about what the data is telling us.

Can you help them make up their minds about these statements?
Complete the table to show what the data is telling them.

Statement	Is certainly true	Is likely to be true	We cannot be sure	Is likely to be false	Is certainly false
A lot of children think the playground is messy.	✓				
A lot of adults agree that the playground is messy.		✓			
There are some bins.					
More bins would help.					
Children do not care about the environment.					
The playground is too windy.					
Banning snacks with wrappers could help.					

Peer feedback

Show your table to a different partner and ask them to tell you ...

Two things that they agree with you about (write what they tell you here):

 ....

⭐ ....

One thing that they think you could have done better (write what they tell you and if you agree with them here):

🌠 ....

Independent reflection activity

Check your learning goals

If you are sure you have met them and can give a reason why put a '★'.

If you think you have met them put a '☺'.

If you think you are not quite there yet put a '☺'.

6

Developing research skills: Lesson 6

Research learning objectives

1.3 Conducting research

1.4 Recording findings

Lesson learning goals

These are the goals for this lesson.
You will return to this table at the end of the lesson for the independent reflection activity.

My learning goals To develop my knowledge and understanding about:	I think	My teacher/ partner thinks
how to conduct a survey and record my findings using a tally chart		
how to interpret the results of a questionnaire		
how to look at results and use them to see if my prediction was accurate		

Prior learning

Look back to Lesson 1 of this unit.

1   What was the name of the global issue that you decided matters in your home area?
2   What did you decide were some of the problems it causes?

Starter activity

The topic I am working on today is:

....

Working in your group, discuss why you think this problem is happening. List some possible reasons below:

The problem:

....

Possible reasons:

....

....

....

....

....

....

Main activity

Your group is going to carry out an investigation to find out what other people think about the problem. Make some predictions about what you think the results will be.

Write your predictions here:

....

Use the reasons that you thought of in the starter activity to make three statements about the causes of your problem.

Step 1: Write the three statements in the table below.

Step 2: Ask others what they think of the statements.

Step 3: Record their answers in the table by tallying.

Statement 1:				
Strongly agree	**Agree**	**Do not know**	**Disagree**	**Strongly disagree**

Statement 2:				
Strongly agree	**Agree**	**Do not know**	**Disagree**	**Strongly disagree**

Statement 3:				
Strongly agree	**Agree**	**Do not know**	**Disagree**	**Strongly disagree**

1   What have you learnt from carrying out your investigation?

....

....

2   Which of your predictions is correct?

....

....

3   How could you present the results of your investigation?

....

....

Independent reflection activity

Check your learning goals

If you are sure you have met them and can give a reason why put a '★'.

If you think you have met them put a '☺'.

If you think you are not quite there yet put a '☹'.

Self-assessment Lessons 4–6

How will I know if I have achieved my learning goals?

Use this activity to reflect on how well you have progressed over the last three lessons.

Tick (✓) 'Achieved' if you are sure you have made good progress with this skill and can give an example.

Tick (✓) 'Not there yet / with help' if you need some further practice so that you can make more progress.

If you tick 'Achieved', then challenge yourself to make further progress in the next section.

If you tick 'Not there yet / with help', there will be the chance to consolidate this skill in future lessons.

Research learning objectives — To develop my knowledge and understanding about:	Not there yet / with help	Achieved	Example
constructing research questions			
information skills			
conducting research			
recording findings			

Continued

Reflect on your responses in your self-assessment and identify one area for improvement.

One area I want to improve in is:

....

How I will improve:

....

Challenge topic review

Think about the Challenge topic you have been exploring and complete the following statements.

I was surprised to discover/explore that ....

....

I did not know ....

....

I now think ....

....

7

Getting better at research skills: Lesson 7

Research learning objectives

1.3 Conducting research

1.4 Recording findings

Lesson learning goals

These are the goals for this lesson.
You will return to this table at the end of the lesson for the independent reflection activity.

My learning goals To get better at:	I think	My teacher/ partner thinks
deciding whether a prediction is correct as a result of carrying out an investigation		
giving reasons for choosing a way of selecting, organising and recording information from a source		

Prior learning

Which of these are predictions?

		Prediction (✓)
1	Our team is going to win the championship this year.	
2	Over 2 000 people went to the swimming pool yesterday.	
3	If more people used public transport, there would be fewer traffic jams.	
4	I think our survey will show that most people prefer chocolate.	
5	The library closes at 5 o'clock on Wednesdays.	

Check with a partner to see if you agree. How do you know it is a prediction?

Starter activity

Read the following two paragraphs:

Scientists say that when children do not drink enough, they become dehydrated. As a result, it becomes harder for them to concentrate on their lessons, they feel tired and they may also suffer from headaches and dizziness.

At Arun and Sofia's school, there are drinking fountains on the playground and in the school corridors. In addition, children are allowed to bring their own drinks from home. They have to keep these in their school bags, and they are only available at break times.

Class discussion

1 What can schools do to stop children becoming dehydrated?
2 How do you prefer to stay hydrated while you are at school?
3 What are the advantages and disadvantages of the system at Arun and Sofia's school?

Main activity part 1

The topic I am working on today is:

....

Arun and Sofia are going to carry out an investigation. They want to find out what changes their classmates would like to make to this system.

They discuss what changes they think would be most popular.

> I think most children would prefer to keep their own drink with them at all times, even during lessons.

> I do not think the school would agree to that. Some children bring unhealthy sugary drinks with them.

> OK, so maybe they would be happy to drink only water, if they could have it with them all the time.

As a result of their discussion, Sofia and Arun make this prediction:

Most children would prefer to drink only water at school, so long as it is available at all times.

Class discussion

1   How could Arun and Sofia check to see if their prediction is correct?
2   What questions do you think they should ask?

Main activity part 2

This is the questionnaire Arun and Sofia use in their investigation:

HYDRATION QUESTIONNAIRE

Currently, it is a school rule that pupils can only have a drink at break times.

1   Are you happy with the current system at our school?   YES/NO

2   If you answered 'No' to Question 1, which of these changes would you prefer?

  a   to be allowed to go to the drinking fountain at all times?

  OR

  b   to have your own drink with you at all times?

3   If you answered 'b' to Question 2, would you change your mind if you
  could only have water to drink?   YES/NO

In their survey, Arun and Sofia ask 20 children to complete the questionnaire.
They use a bar chart to show their results:

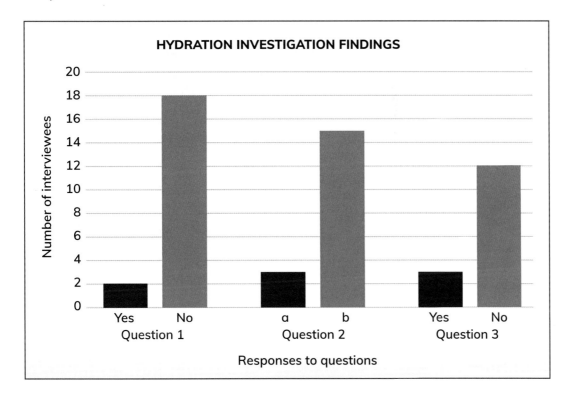

Class discussion

1   Was the prediction correct? How do you know?

2   Why do you think Sofia and Arun chose a bar chart to show their results?

3   How could Sofia and Arun use these results to bring about change in their school?

Independent reflection activity

Check your learning goals

If you are sure you have met them and can give a reason why put a '★'.

If you think you have met them put a '☺'.

If you think you are not quite there yet put a '☺'.

8

Getting better at research skills: Lesson 8

Research learning objectives

1.1 Constructing research questions

1.2 Information skills

Lesson learning goals

These are the goals for this lesson.
You will return to this table at the end of the lesson for the independent reflection activity.

My learning goals To get better at:	I think	My teacher/ partner thinks
understanding what makes a global and local issue		
making my own questions in order to understand global and local issues		
identifying useful sources for finding answers to my questions		

Prior learning

1   What comes to mind now when you think of 'global issues'?

2   How do they have an impact in your area?

Have a discussion.
Take turns to say what you think the most important global issues are to you and what their local impact is.

Starter activity

It can be useful when we are researching local and global issues to think about causes and consequences.

The list below has got jumbled up – global issues, causes and consequences are all mixed up. Can you sort it out? The first one has been done for you. Cross them off as you work through.

People can do their shopping online; Polar ice caps are melting; Local shops go out of business; ~~Greenhouse gases are released;~~ People have to reduce the amount they use; Children eat too much sugar; Sea levels are rising; There is not enough water; Children become obese; ~~Coal is burnt to produce electricity.~~

Issue	Cause	Consequence
Energy	Coal is burnt to produce electricity.	Greenhouse gases are released.
Technology		
Water		
Climate change		
Food		

Class discussion

1   What local consequences do these global issues have in our area?
2   What can be done about these local consequences?
3   How can we find out more about the local consequences?

Main activity

Thinking about the causes and consequences of an issue can help you to develop questions with a good focus. In the end, you want to be able to take an action that will make a positive change.

Zara and Marcus have been thinking about the causes and consequences of local traffic problems in their area to come up with questions. They used a mind-map to organise their ideas. They have put a * next to questions that would help them take action.

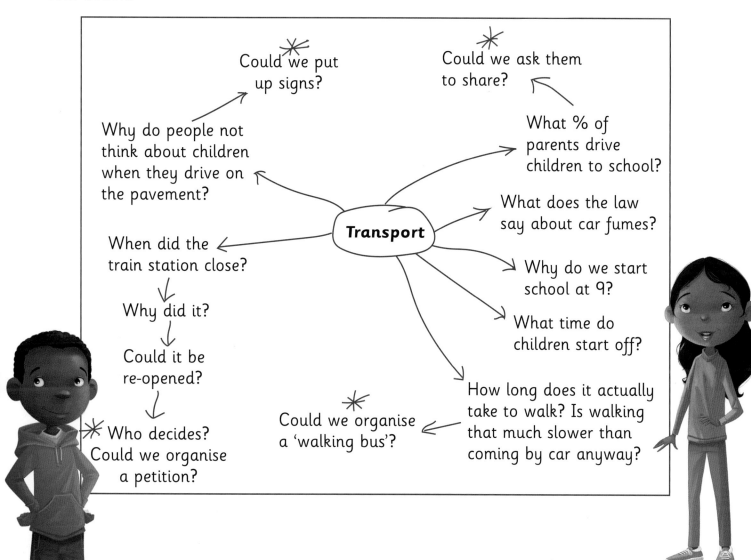

The topic I am working on today is:

....

Now think of an issue in your area and come up with some questions.
You can use a mind-map like Zara and Marcus. Put a * next to questions
that would help you take action.

What sources could you use to find the answers to your questions?
Add this information to your mind-map.

Peer feedback

Ask a partner to look at your mind-map and to tell you the answers to these questions:

- Is the issue important in your area?   YES/NO

- Does the mind-map include three or more questions about the issue?   YES/NO

- For each question, is there a source that will help to find the answer?   YES/NO

Independent reflection activity

Check your learning goals

If you are sure you have met them and can give a reason why put a '★'.

If you think you have met them put a '☺'.

If you think you are not quite there yet put a '☺'.

Getting better at research skills: Lesson 9

Research learning objectives

1.2 Information skills

1.3 Conducting research

1.4 Recording findings

Lesson learning goals

These are the goals for this lesson.
You will return to this table at the end of the lesson for the independent reflection activity.

My learning goals To get better at:	I think	My teacher/ partner thinks
giving reasons for choosing a source to help me find out about a topic		
deciding whether a prediction is correct as a result of carrying out an investigation		
choosing a way of clearly showing what I have learnt from my research		

Prior learning

Marcus and Sofia are doing research into why children travel to school by car. They would like to reduce the number of journeys made by car, to reduce air pollution near their school.

Which of the following do you think would be the most useful things for them to do? Put them in order from 1 (most useful) to 6 (least useful).

- Carry out a survey to find out how many children travel to school by car.

- Find out what other schools are doing about the problem of air pollution.

- Look at a local map to see where children live, and how far they have to travel.

- Observe children arriving at school in the morning.

- Talk to children about what they think is the best way to travel to school.

- Talk to parents to find out why they bring their children to school by car.

Look at the one you have chosen as 'most useful' and tell a partner why you think this.

Starter activity

Zara and Arun have carried out an investigation to find out if the distance that families live from the school is important when it comes to choosing a way to travel to school.

Before the investigation, Zara made a prediction:

'The further away a family lives, the more likely they are to travel to school by car.'

Zara and Arun chose different ways to present what they found out from the investigation.

Zara: 'I showed our results using a bar chart.'

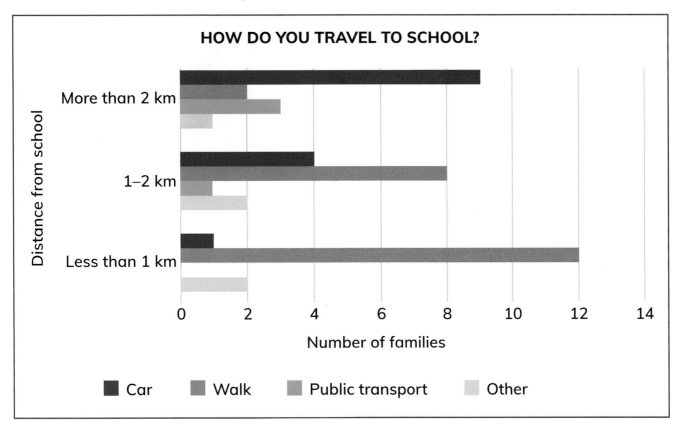

HOW DO YOU TRAVEL TO SCHOOL?

Legend: ■ Car ■ Walk ■ Public transport ▨ Other

Arun: 'I put our results into a table.'

Distance from school	Method of travelling			
	Car	Walk	Public transport (e.g. bus)	Other (e.g. bike)
More than 2 km	9	2	3	1
1–2 km	4	8	1	2
Less than 1 km	1	12	0	2

Class discussion

1 Which way of presenting the results do you prefer, and why?
2 Is Zara's prediction correct? How do you know?

3 What action could Zara and Arun now take? Here are a couple of suggestions:

Zara: 'We could ask people to share their cars, so they take fewer journeys.'

Arun: 'Why don't we try to persuade more people to use public transport?'

Main activity

The topic I am working on today is:

....

In your group, think of something that you would like to change in your local environment.

1 What would you like to change?

....

2 Why would you like to change it?

....

3 What changes could be made?

....

4 Make a prediction about which type of change would be most popular, and why.

....

5 Write some questions you could ask to find out if your prediction is correct.

....

6 What sources could you use in your investigation?

....

7 What method would you use to show your results, and why?

....

Independent reflection activity

Check your learning goals

If you are sure you have met them and can give a reason why put a '★'.

If you think you have met them put a '☺'.

If you think you are not quite there yet put a '☹'.

Self-assessment Lessons 7–9

How will I know if I have achieved my learning goals?

Use this activity to reflect on how well you have progressed over the last three lessons.

Tick (✓) 'Achieved' if you are sure you have made good progress with this skill and can give an example.

Tick (✓) 'Not there yet / with help' if you need some further practice so that you can make more progress.

If you tick 'Achieved', then challenge yourself to make further progress in the next section.

If you tick 'Not there yet / with help', there will be the chance to consolidate this skill in future lessons.

Research learning objectives To get better at:	Not there yet / with help	Achieved	Example
constructing research questions			
constructing research questions			
conducting research			
recording findings			

Continued

Reflect on your responses in your self-assessment and identify one area for improvement.

One area I want to improve in is:

....

How I will improve:

....

Challenge topic review

Think about the Challenge topic you have been exploring and complete the following statements.

I was surprised to discover/explore that ....

....

I did not know ....

....

I now think ....

....

community garden

Starting with analysis skills: Lesson 1

Analysis learning objectives

2.1 Identifying perspectives

Lesson learning goals

These are the goals for this lesson.
You will return to this table at the end of the lesson for the independent reflection activity.

My learning goals To start to:	I think	My teacher/ partner thinks
recognise that there are differences in the ways different people think about a topic		

Prior learning

1   Make five pairs of words from the words in this list:

   cause   global   opinion   problem   result

   solution   prediction   local   **fact**   consequence

2   What is the connection between the words in each pair?
    Explain to a partner.

Starter activity

A perspective is a way of looking at a topic.

Everyone can have a **personal** perspective, which is their own individual way of looking at a topic.

Zara and Sofia have different personal perspectives on a topic.

Well, I think it's cruel to animals, so I have stopped doing it.

I know what you mean, but I like the taste so much I would find it hard to give it up.

Class discussion

1   What topic do you think they are talking about?

2   What is your personal perspective on this topic? Is it the same as Zara's or Sofia's, or is it something different?

3   Why do you think different people have different perspectives on a topic?

Here are some more topics:

| litter | public transport | video games | climate change |

Choose **one** of these topics. Write it in the first column in the table below:

Topic	My personal perspective	Different personal perspectives
....	....	....
....	....	....
....	....	....

1   What is your personal perspective on this topic?
    Write it in the middle column in the table.

2   Now ask other people about their personal perspective on this topic.
    Is it the same as yours, or is it different?
    If it is different, make a note of it in the right-hand column.

Listen carefully to people whose perspective is different to yours.
Could it make you change your own perspective?

Main activity part 1

The topic I am working on today is:

....

As well as personal perspectives, there can be local or national perspectives
(looking at something from the point of view of a particular place or country)
and global perspectives (looking at the way something affects people from
many different countries, or our planet).

Here are some different perspectives on the same topic:

A   Exporting more meat overseas will mean that we can
    afford to build more schools and hospitals.

B   Raising animals for meat production is a major source
    of greenhouse gases, causing climate change.

C   I have been feeling a lot healthier since I stopped eating
    burgers every day.

Class discussion

Which is a personal perspective, which is a local or national
perspective, and which is a global perspective? How do you know?

Main activity part 2

Now look again at the personal perspectives you wrote in the starter activity
about the topic of litter, public transport, video games or climate change.

1   Write the topic you chose in the 'Topic' column of the table below.

2   Choose one personal perspective (either your own or someone else's) on the topic you chose and write it in the 'Personal' column.

3   How does this topic affect people in your local area or in your country? Write a local or national perspective in the third column.

4   How does this topic affect our planet, or people all around the world? Write a global perspective in the final column.

Topic	Personal	Local/national	Global
....	....	....	....
....	....	....	....
....	....	....	....

Peer feedback

Show your work to a partner and ask them to tell you the answers to these questions:

1   Are all three perspectives about the same topic?   YES/NO

2   Do you agree that the local or national perspective is about how the topic affects people in your local area or country?   YES/NO

3   Does the global perspective show how this topic affects our planet, or people around the world?   YES/NO

Independent reflection activity

Check your learning goals

If you are sure you have met them and can give a reason why put a '★'.

If you think you have met them put a '☺'.

If you think you are not quite there yet put a '☺'.

2

Starting with analysis skills: Lesson 2

Analysis learning objectives

2.3 Making connections

2.4 Solving problems

Lesson learning goals		
These are the goals for this lesson. You will return to this table at the end of the lesson for the independent reflection activity.		

My learning goals To start to:	I think	My teacher/ partner thinks
talk about problems that affect people where I live and what causes them		
talk about how a local problem affects me and other people, and what can be done about it		

Prior learning

Here are some different perspectives on a problem at Sofia's school.
Sort the perspectives into three groups: personal, local/national and global.

Perspective	Personal	Local/ National	Global
a They should not show advertisements for unhealthy snacks on TV when children like me are watching.			
b In this generation, more young people are suffering problems such as obesity because of an unhealthy diet.			
c Many small shopkeepers in the area rely on children buying sweets and snacks from their shops.			
d Plastic used for packaging of sweets and snacks often cannot be recycled, and causes environmental pollution.			
e This school encourages its learners to bring healthy snacks from home in reusable containers.			
f My friends and I buy sweets and sugary snacks because we think they taste great.			

Talk with a partner:

1   What is the problem?
2   What do you think are the causes of the problem?
3   What are its consequences?
4   What could the solution be?

Starter activity

The children are discussing some other problems that affect them
at their school or in their neighbourhood.

Children have to play in the sun at breaktime when the weather's hot.

We spend too long queuing up for our food at lunchtime.

There are always traffic jams outside the school when parents are dropping their children off or picking them up.

We have to carry too many books to and from school every day.

Your teacher will give you one of these problems to talk about in your group.

Discuss the answers to these questions with the others in your group:

1   What are the possible causes of the problem?

2   How could the problem affect children at the school?

3   What solutions could there be to the problem?

Class discussion

Report to the class the answers to the questions you have discussed in your group.

Which problem do you think is the most important, and why?

Main activity

The topic I am working on today is:

....

Use the template your teacher gives you to make a mind-map of some problems that affect you and other people at your school or in your neighbourhood.
Think about these questions:

For each problem you think of:

- What are its causes?
- Who does it affect, and how?
- What solutions to the problem are there?

1 Look at your mind-map, and with your other group members, agree on the problem that you think is the most important:

....

....

2 What is your personal perspective on this problem?

....

....

....

3 What other perspectives on this problem are there among people in your group?

....

....

....

4   What other perspectives on this problem are there among people in your school or neighbourhood?

....

....

....

5   What are other people doing to try and solve this problem?

....

....

....

6   What do you think is the best solution to the problem, and why?

....

....

....

Report back to the class on the work you have done.

Independent reflection activity

Check your learning goals

If you are sure you have met them and can give a reason why put a '★'.

If you think you have met them put a '☺'.

If you think you are not quite there yet put a '☹'.

Starting with analysis skills: Lesson 3

Analysis learning objectives

2.2 Interpreting data

Lesson learning goals
These are the goals for this lesson. You will return to this table at the end of the lesson for the independent reflection activity.

My learning goals To start to:	I think	My teacher/ partner thinks
find and describe patterns in data and say what they mean		

Prior learning

Match each of the problems to a solution.
One example has been done for you.

Problem	Solution
Air pollution in our cities is causing health problems.	Ban advertisements for fast food from prime-time TV.
Mass tourism is making life difficult for local residents.	Make public transport cheaper and faster.
More and more young people are becoming obese.	Encourage people to buy re-usable water bottles.
Plastic waste is polluting our rivers and oceans.	Limit the number of people allowed to visit at any one time.

Talk with a partner.

1 Which of the problems affect people where you live?
2 What other solutions could there be for each problem?

Starter activity

Study the graph on the next page. It shows you the average maximum and minimum daily temperatures for each month where Sofia lives.

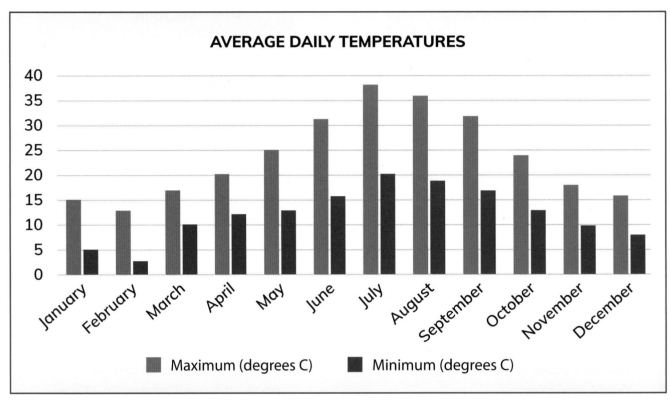

AVERAGE DAILY TEMPERATURES

Maximum (degrees C)   Minimum (degrees C)

Class discussion

1   What patterns can you see in the data presented in the chart?
2   How might these patterns affect what Sofia and her friends do at different times of the year?

Main activity

The topic I am working on today is:

....

At Sofia's school, there are three terms: August–December, January–March, April–June.

During Term 3 (April–June), the school carried out an investigation into how children travel to school. These are the results:

Number of children travelling:	April	May	June
by car	154	193	227
by public transport	45	42	47
on foot	236	205	163
other	10	6	7
Total	445	446	444

In your group, talk about what these results show you.

1   Can you see any patterns in the data? Look for anything that changes in a regular way, month by month, by reading across the columns.

   ....

2   What could explain these patterns? Look again at the chart showing average temperatures. Is there a connection between the two sets of data?

   ....

The school carried out a second investigation in Term 1. Here are the findings:

Number of children travelling:	September	October	November
by car	235	192	164
by public transport	46	41	43
on foot	157	202	228
other	8	11	9
Total	446	446	444

Talk about what these results show you.

1   Can you see any patterns in the data?

    ....

2   What could explain these patterns?

    ....

Class discussion

1   What overall conclusion can you draw from the data?
2   Sofia and her friends want to encourage more children to walk to school. How could they use this data to achieve that goal?

Independent reflection activity

Check your learning goals

If you are sure you have met them and can give a reason why put a '★'.

If you think you have met them put a '☺'.

If you think you are not quite there yet put a '☺'.

Self-assessment Lessons 1–3

How will I know if I have achieved my learning goals?

Use this activity to reflect on how well you have progressed over the last three lessons.

Tick (✓) 'Achieved' if you are sure you have made good progress with this skill and can give an example.

Tick (✓) 'Not there yet / with help' if you need some further practice so that you can make more progress.

If you tick 'Achieved', then challenge yourself to make further progress in the next section.

If you tick 'Not there yet / with help', there will be the chance to consolidate this skill in future lessons.

Continued

Analysis learning objectives To start to:	Not there yet / with help	Achieved	Example
identify perspectives			
interpret data			
make connections			
solve problems			

Reflect on your responses in your self-assessment and identify one area for improvement.

One area I want to improve in is:

....

How I will improve:

....

Challenge topic review

Think about the Challenge topic you have been exploring and complete the following statements.

I was surprised to discover/explore that ....

....

I did not know ....

....

I now think ....

....

Developing analysis skills: Lesson 4

Analysis learning objectives

2.1 Identifying perspectives

Lesson learning goals		
These are the goals for this lesson. You will return to this table at the end of the lesson for the independent reflection activity.		
My learning goals **To develop my knowledge and understanding about:**	I think	My teacher/ partner thinks
describing how different people – including myself – think and feel about a topic		

Prior learning

Here are four perspectives on the topic of air travel:

A Everyone in my family is happy that the new airport is opening because it means there will be jobs for all of us.

B Many hotels in this country are closing down because people prefer to fly abroad for their holidays.

C The noise of the planes taking off and landing at the airport keeps me awake at night.

D If people stopped flying, fewer tourists would visit our island and this would have a negative effect on the economy.

Decide where in this grid to put each perspective.
Write the letter in the correct box in the grid.

Air travel	Personal perspective	Local/national perspective
For		
Against		

Talk with a partner.

What global perspectives on air travel can you think of?

Starter activity

Read this short article:

> On the Southerly Islands, the climate is warm and wet, which means that farmers can grow flowers in their fields all year round. Local workers pick the flowers by hand and they are then flown by plane to be sold thousands of kilometres away in Northland, where the climate is too cold to grow flowers outdoors for much of the year.

Now look at these different perspectives on the flower trade and match them to the people. One has been done for you.

Perspective		Who?
The work is poorly paid and back-breaking, but the farmers do not care so long as they make a profit.		A consumer in Northland
I love being able to buy exotic and colourful flowers at any time of year – they are perfect for special occasions.		A technology expert
Moving people and goods by air is contributing to climate change because of all the carbon that is released.		A farmer in the Southerly Islands
Although our flowers are local, they cost more to produce because we have to grow them indoors.		An environmental campaigner
Transporting flowers by air is costly – if we had to pay our workers more, we would go out of business, and they would be out of a job.		A farm worker on the Southerly Islands
The work could be done by machines, but the farmers will not invest in them – they prefer to pay their workers as little as possible.		A flower-grower in Northland

Class discussion

1 Who is in favour of the trade and why?
2 Who is against the trade? Why?
3 What other perspectives on the flower trade could there be?
4 What is your personal perspective on this topic? Why do you think or feel that way?

Main activity

The topic I am working on today is:

....

Stakeholders are people who have an interest in a topic – they may be for or against it, have some control or influence over it, or be in some way affected by it. The people in the list in the Starter activity are all stakeholders in the flower trade between the Southerly Islands and Northland.

Think about another topic (for example, using public transport or playing video games). Who are the stakeholders? Use the template of a mind-map that your teacher gives you to focus your ideas.

Choose two of the stakeholders from your mind-map. Each of them should have a different perspective on this topic. Is it positive or negative?

1   Stakeholder 1's perspective:

....

2   Stakeholder 2's perspective:

....

3   What is your own personal perspective on the topic?

....

4   Why do you think or feel that way about it?

....

Share your ideas by reporting back to the whole class.

Independent reflection activity

Check your learning goals

If you are sure you have met them and can give a reason why put a '★'.

If you think you have met them put a '☺'.

If you think you are not quite there yet put a '☺'.

Developing analysis skills: Lesson 5

Analysis learning objectives

2.3 Making connections

2.4 Solving problems

Lesson learning goals

These are the goals for this lesson.
You will return to this table at the end of the lesson for the independent reflection activity.

My learning goals To develop my knowledge and understanding about:	I think	My teacher/ partner thinks
explaining the causes of local problems and how they affect people		
discussing the actions I could take to help solve a local problem		

Prior learning

For each of these **issues**, find a cause, a consequence and a solution and write its letter in the appropriate box in the grid.

Issue	Cause	Consequence	Solution
Noise pollution			
Plastic pollution			
Air pollution			

A People throwing away bottles, bags and packaging	B Local residents have sleepless nights	C Improve public transport
D Ban night-time flights	E Drivers using their cars in the city centre	F More and more litter in the environment
G City residents develop health problems	H Set up recycling centres	I Planes taking off and landing at nearby airport

Talk with a partner.

1   What other consequences could there be?

2   What other solutions could be found?

Starter activity

Arun and his classmates have been discussing the problem of air pollution, which affects their school mainly because of the heavy traffic on the street outside. They have suggested a number of possible actions they could take to help solve this problem:

1 Make a 'No Stopping' zone on the street outside the school to stop parents using their cars to drop off and pick up their children.

2 Put up posters outside the school to make people more aware of the dangers of air pollution.

3 Plant a 'green wall' of trees and bushes in front of the school to absorb some of the pollution.

4 Provide all children with anti-smog masks to wear on their journeys to and from school.

5 Give a presentation to the whole school, including parents, in a special assembly about the dangers of air pollution.

6 Reward children who walk to school or use public transport, using a points system that will earn them prizes.

Class discussion

1 What arguments are there in favour of each of the solutions?

2 What arguments are there against each of the solutions?

3 What other solutions could there be?

4 Which solution do you think would be the most effective and why?

Main activity part 1

The topic I am working on today is:

....

Arun's group have decided that their preferred solution is to provide all children with anti-smog masks.

When Arun and his group propose that the school should provide anti-smog masks for all the children, the school leaders ask him to write a justification for this solution. (When you justify something, you give reasons for it or explain why you have chosen it.)

Read what Arun wrote:

Justification

Research shows that air pollution can cause young people to suffer from health problems such as asthma and lung diseases. Because our school is on a busy road, children are exposed to air pollution, especially during their journeys to and from school. Anti-smog masks can stop up to 90 percent of the particles in the air from entering children's lungs, giving children some protection. At the same time, wearing masks would remind people of the dangers of air pollution, and perhaps make them change their minds about using their cars so often. It would also show that the school cares about the health of its learners.

Class discussion

1   What arguments does Arun use to justify taking action on this issue?
2   What arguments does Arun use to justify the solution of wearing anti-smog masks?

Main activity part 2

Sofia thinks there is a problem with Arun's solution.

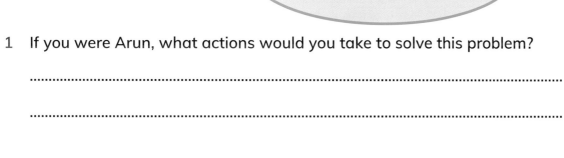

Masks will cost money. The school might not be able to afford them.

1   If you were Arun, what actions would you take to solve this problem?

    ....

    ....

2 What other actions could you take to help solve the problem of air pollution?

....

....

Peer feedback

Show your work to a partner, and ask them to tell you the answers
to these questions:

Does my solution help to solve the problem of paying for the anti-smog masks? YES/NO

Have I thought of other practical ways to solve the problem of air pollution? YES/NO

Independent reflection activity

Check your learning goals

If you are sure you have met them and can give a reason why put a '★'.

If you think you have met them put a '☺'.

If you think you are not quite there yet put a '☹'.

6

Developing analysis skills: Lesson 6

Analysis learning objectives

2.2 Interpreting data

Lesson learning goals

These are the goals for this lesson.
You will return to this table at the end of the lesson for the independent reflection activity.

My learning goals To develop my knowledge and understanding about:	I think	My teacher/ partner thinks
finding patterns in data and explaining what they mean		

Prior learning

Marcus has found some data about how much time people of different ages spend online everyday:

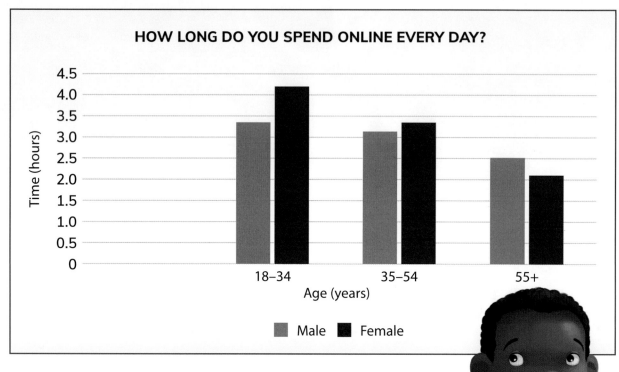

HOW LONG DO YOU SPEND ONLINE EVERY DAY?

Marcus looks for some patterns in the data.

1   Which of his conclusions are correct?

   a   Older people spend less time online.

   b   Women in every age group spend more time online than men.

   c   A typical 30-year-old man spends more time online than a 50-year old woman.

   d   A typical 60-year-old woman spends about half as much time online as a 30-year-old woman.

Talk with a partner:

2   What other conclusions can you draw from this data?

3   What do you think the graph would look like for people in the 10–18 age group? Why do you think that? How could you check your prediction?

Starter activity

Zara has been investigating how people follow the news.
She made a questionnaire:

News questionnaire				
	Yes		**No**	
1 Are you interested in the news?				
	Television	**Online**	**Radio**	**Newspaper**
2 If you answered 'Yes' to Question 1, how do you get the news?				

Use Zara's questionnaire to carry out a quick survey among other learners.

1   What do you predict the result will be?

   ....

2   What do your results show you?

   ....

Class discussion

1   What did you find out from your survey?
2   How accurate was your prediction?
3   How could Zara's questionnaire be improved?
4   Why do some people think it is important to follow the news?

Main activity

The topic I am working on today is:

....

Zara redesigned her questionnaire. With her group, she carried out another investigation into how people follow the news in their local area.
This time, they decided to collect data from children of their own age and their parents.

They recorded their findings in two graphs:

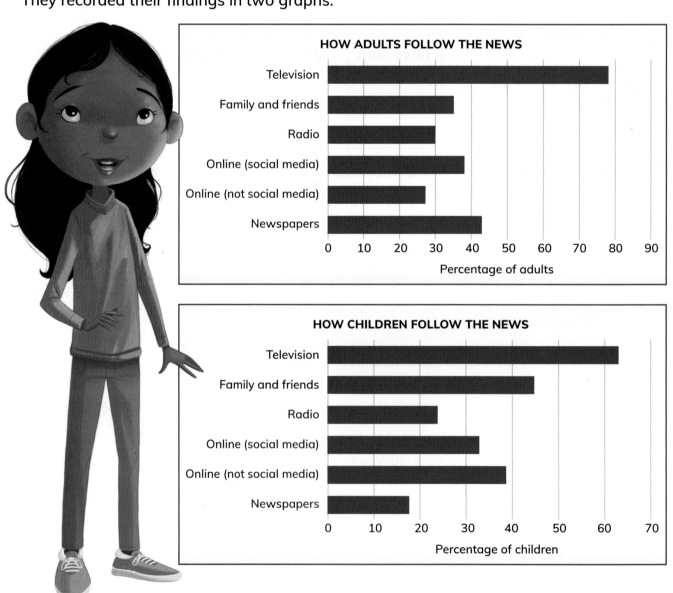

Compare the two sets of data. Working with a partner, write down three things that the data shows you. Find at least one thing that is the same for adults and children, and one thing that is different:

1 ....

2 ....

3 ....

Class discussion

1 What similarities and differences are there in the data for adults and children?

2 What improvements did Zara make to her questionnaire?

3 How could Zara's group use their data to try to persuade more children to take an interest in the news?

Independent reflection activity

Check your learning goals

If you are sure you have met them and can give a reason why put a '★'.

If you think you have met them put a '☺'.

If you think you are not quite there yet put a '☺'.

Self-assessment Lessons 4–6

How will I know if I have achieved my learning goals?

Use this activity to reflect on how well you have progressed over the last three lessons.

Tick (✓) 'Achieved' if you are sure you have made good progress with this skill and can give an example.

Tick (✓) 'Not there yet / with help' if you need some further practice so that you can make more progress.

If you tick 'Achieved', then challenge yourself to make further progress in the next section.

If you tick 'Not there yet / with help', there will be the chance to consolidate this skill in future lessons.

Continued

Analysis learning objectives To develop my knowledge and understanding about:	Not there yet / with help	Achieved	Example
identifying perspectives			
interpreting data			
making connections			
solving problems			

Reflect on your responses in your self-assessment and identify one area for improvement.

One area I want to improve in is:

....

How I will improve:

....

Challenge topic review

Think about the Challenge topic you have been exploring and complete the following statements.

I was surprised to discover/explore that ....

....

I did not know ....

....

I now think ....

....

Getting better at analysis skills: Lesson 7

Analysis learning objectives

2.1 Identifying perspectives

Lesson learning goals		
These are the goals for this lesson. You will return to this table at the end of the lesson for the independent reflection activity.		
My learning goals **To get better at:**	I think	My teacher/ partner thinks
identifying some different ways that people can think about an issue		
recognising words that show the strength of feeling about an issue		

Prior learning

How would you score yourself in answer to the following statements?
Tick (✓) the answer that best applies to you:

1 I know what issue I will be taking action on.

Very clear	Quite clear	Some idea	Not very clear	Not at all clear

2 I know what my goal is.

Very clear	Quite clear	Some idea	Not very clear	Not at all clear

3 I know what other people think about the issue.

Very clear	Quite clear	Some idea	Not very clear	Not at all clear

Hold a class discussion: How could we improve our scores?

Starter activity

Your teacher will give you some different perspectives on the flower trade. How would you categorise them? The first one has been done for you.

Perspective	Strongly against	Somewhat against	Neutral	Somewhat in favour	Strongly in favour
1	✓				
2					
3					
4					
5					
6					

Class discussion

Look at your answers in the starter activity and discuss these questions:

1. How did you recognise an argument that was strongly against the trade?
2. What words or phrases did they use to emphasise the strength of their feelings?
3. How did you recognise an argument that was strongly in favour of the trade?
4. What words or phrases did they use to emphasise the strength of their feelings?
5. What words or phrases could you use to emphasise the strength of your feelings about your issue?

Main activity

The topic I am working on today is:

....

Look back and choose two of the stakeholders you identified in Lesson 4.
Each had a different perspective on an issue.

1. What was the issue?

   ....

   ....

2. What was stakeholder 1's perspective?

   ....

3. What facts could stakeholder 1 use to convince someone to support their perspective?

   ....

4. What words or phrases could stakeholder 1 use to convince someone that they ought to care about the issue?

   ....

5. What was stakeholder 2's perspective?

   ....

6   What facts could stakeholder 2 use to convince someone to support their perspective?

....

7   What words or phrases could stakeholder 2 use to convince someone that they ought to care about the issue?

....

Peer feedback

Pretend you are one of the stakeholders and try to convince your partner to support your perspective. Ask them to tell you …

Two things that they like about your persuasive powers (write what they tell you here):

★ ....

★ ....

One thing that you could do better (write what they tell you here):

 ....

Independent reflection activity

Check your learning goals

If you are sure you have met them and can give a reason why put a '★'.

If you think you have met them put a '☺'.

If you think you are not quite there yet put a '☹'.

8

Getting better at analysis skills: Lesson 8

Analysis learning objectives

2.3 Making connections

2.4 Solving problems

Lesson learning goals		
These are the goals for this lesson. You will return to this table at the end of the lesson for the independent reflection activity.		
My learning goals To get better at:	I think	My teacher/ partner thinks
developing ideas about how I would solve a local problem		
considering pros and cons for different people about ways to solve a local problem		

Prior learning

Marcus has been writing:

My issue is transport to school. I think that children should have a safe place to store their bikes at school. I feel passionate about this because I love cycling, and I really don't enjoy the walk to school every day on the noisy street. I know that when children cycle to school, it cuts down significantly on traffic and reduces air pollution.

Prepare your ideas for a class discussion.

1   What is Marcus's issue?
2   What is Marcus's perspective about the issue?
3   What does he think should be done?
4   Why does he think or feel this way?
5   What facts have made him think or feel this way?
6   If he wanted to convince someone else to support his perspective, what could he say?

Be ready to justify your ideas.

Starter activity

1   What is your issue?

   ....

2   What is your own personal perspective about the issue?
    How do you feel about it?

   ....

3   What do you think should be done?

   ....

4   Why do you think or feel this way?

   ....

5   What facts have made you think or feel this way?

   ....

6   If you wanted to convince someone else to support your perspective,
    what would your key points be?

    ....

    ....

    ....

    ....

Main activity

Your teacher will introduce an issue and a possible solution. This will help you
to consider the way in which this solution might impact on different people.

Now it is your turn. Choose a local problem and, with other members of your
group, think of a possible solution. Consider the impacts on different groups
of people of the solution.

The topic I am working on today is:

....

The problem:					
Solution	Impact on younger children	Impact on older children	Impact on parents	Impact on staff at school	Impact on other people in the community

Class discussion

Record your thoughts for a class discussion.

1   Whose perspectives would probably be favourable to your solution?

    ....

2   Would your solution be effective?

    ....

3   How would this solution change the way different groups of people
    might have to behave?

    ....

    ....

4   How could you justify your solution to people who might not want to
    change the way they behave at first? (Think about different global
    and local perspectives on the problem.)

    ....

    ....

    ....

Class discussion

Be ready to report back to the class about your solution,
how it would work, and how you would justify it.

Independent reflection activity

Check your learning goals

If you are sure you have met them and can give a reason why put a '★'.

If you think you have met them put a '☺'.

If you think you are not quite there yet put a '☺'.

9

Getting better at analysis skills: Lesson 9

Analysis learning objectives

2.1 Identifying perspectives

2.2 Interpreting data

2.3 Making connections

2.4 Solving problems

Lesson learning goals		
These are the goals for this lesson. You will return to this table at the end of the lesson for the independent reflection activity.		
My learning goals To get better at:	I think	My teacher/ partner thinks
describing in some detail the differences in the ways people think about a topic		
saying how other people's ways of thinking about a topic differ from my own, and why		
using a pattern found in data to support an argument and explaining why		
finding connections between local and global problems		

Prior learning

Look back to Zara's group's data in Lesson 6 about how children and adults follow the news.

Here are some statements about the data. Can you classify them?
Put 'T' against any statements that you think are true.
Put 'PT' against any that you think are possibly true. Put 'F' against any that you think are false.

a   Nearly 80 percent of adults follow the news on television.

b   Children do not read newspapers.

c   More adults than children surveyed follow the news on the radio.

d   A greater proportion of children than adults follow the news through family and friends.

e   A greater proportion of children than adults surveyed follow the news online.

Starter activity

Zara's group also conducted a survey about their transport issue. They asked 55 younger children, 52 older children, 29 parents and 19 staff which solution they favoured.

Solution	Younger children	Older children	Parents	Staff	Total in favour
1 Make a 'No Stopping' zone on the street outside the school to stop parents using their cars to drop off and pick up their children.	5	2	4	4	15
2 Put up posters outside the school to make people more aware of the dangers of air pollution.	10	8	2	4	24
3 Plant a 'green wall' of trees and bushes in front of the school to absorb some of the pollution.	14	8	3	5	30
4 Provide all children with anti-smog masks to wear on their journeys to and from school.	5	14	6	1	26

Solution	Younger children	Older children	Parents	Staff	Total in favour
5 Give a presentation to the whole school, including parents, in a special assembly about the dangers of air pollution.	1	4	9	2	16
6 Reward children who walk to school or use public transport, using a points system that will earn them prizes.	20	16	5	3	44
Total surveyed	55	52	29	19	155

What do we know for sure from the survey results?

What conclusions can we reasonably draw? Add your ideas to the table:

We know for sure that ...	We can reasonably conclude that ...
Rewarding children who walk to school or use public transport was the most popular solution.	The children surveyed like getting prizes.

Class discussion

Share your thoughts with the class about what you know for sure, and what you can reasonably conclude.

Main activity

Arun, Zara, Sofia and Marcus have been discussing the results of their data and using it to decide what they should do next. You can read their ideas in the download your teacher will give you.

Use the table below to analyse their suggestions.
The first one has been done for you.

Name	Gave a global reason for their action	Considered different local perspectives	Used a range of detailed research	Considered potential strengths of the action	Considered potential weaknesses of the action
Zara	✗	✗	✗	✗	✓
Arun					
Marcus					
Sofia					

Now *either* write a justification for the action you are considering as part of your challenge or write a justification for the action you think Arun, Zara, Sofia and Marcus should take.

....

....

The topic I am working on today is:

....

My proposed action is

....

This action would be a positive change because

....

I know that different people would benefit from this action because

....

The benefits of this approach are that firstly,

....

In addition,

....

There are, however, limitations to this approach because

....

However, overall, it can be seen that

....

Independent reflection activity

Check your learning goals

If you are sure you have met them and can give a reason why put a '★'.

If you think you have met them put a '☺'.

If you think you are not quite there yet put a '☺'.

Self-assessment Lessons 7–9

How will I know if I have achieved my learning goals?

Use this activity to reflect on how well you have progressed over the last three lessons.

Tick (✓) 'Achieved' if you are sure you have made good progress with this skill and can give an example.

Tick (✓) 'Not there yet / with help' if you need some further practice so that you can make more progress.

If you tick 'Achieved', then challenge yourself to make further progress in the next section.

If you tick 'Not there yet / with help', there will be the chance to consolidate this skill in future lessons.

Continued

Analysis learning objectives To get better at:	Not there yet / with help	Achieved	Example
identifying perspectives			
interpreting data			
making connections			
solving problems			

Reflect on your responses in your self-assessment and identify one area for improvement.

One area I want to improve in is:

....

How I will improve:

....

Challenge topic review

Think about the Challenge topic you have been exploring and complete the following statements.

I was surprised to discover/explore that ....

....

I did not know ....

....

I now think ....

....

1

Starting with evaluation skills: Lesson 1

Evaluation learning objectives

3.1 Evaluating sources

Lesson learning goals		
These are the goals for this lesson. You will return to this table at the end of the lesson for the independent reflection activity.		
My learning goals To start to:	I think	My teacher/ partner thinks
say what the purpose of a source is		
describe some of the features of the source		
recognise why a source may be useful		

Prior learning

Sofia has been thinking about sources of information she has used in different subjects. She has been thinking about where to get facts and perspectives from.

Source	Subject	Could it give us facts?	Could it give us perspectives?
The Natural World book	Science	Yes (e.g. about the water cycle).	Sometimes (e.g. people used to ridicule Copernicus' ideas).
[My Country] in the 19th Century	History	Yes (e.g. dates of key events).	Yes (e.g. different about the causes of events).
Junior Atlas	Geography	Yes (e.g. rainfall statistics).	Not really.
Improve your skills video	PE	Yes (e.g. rules of the game).	Yes (e.g. the coach had ideas about the best technique).

1   What sources of information have you used?

2   Which sources of information have given you facts?

3   Which sources of information have given you perspectives?

4   Which sources of information have given you both facts and perspectives?

5   Make a table like Sofia.

6   Compare your table with a partner.

7   Be ready to share your ideas in the class discussion.

The topic I am working on today is:

....

Starter activity

Can you match the source to its purpose? The first one has been done for you.

Source	Purpose
a page in a geography text book (e.g. about volcanoes)	to outline the characteristics of something, (e.g. 'dinosaurs', 'ancient Benin')
a pamphlet from a campaign group	to change people's minds about something
a sewing or knitting pattern	to explain how or why something happens
an article giving a balanced account of both sides of an issue (e.g. for/against)	to tell someone how to make something
an encyclopedia entry	to give arguments and information from different points of view

Main activity

Zara's Cambridge Global Perspectives topic this term is 'Keeping healthy'. She is worried that not everyone in her class is clear about healthy eating. Her goals are to raise awareness about healthy eating, and give her class some ideas about new food and drink they have not tried. She has been collecting some sources that might be useful. She has also been thinking about their features and how they might be useful.

Look at the sources and their features in the table below.
How do you think they could be useful to Zara?
Add your ideas to the table. The first one has been done for you.

Source	Features	Useful because ...?
Recipe for an avocado smoothie	• Starts with a list of ingredients • Step-by-step photos • Tells you what to do in order	Zara's group could use the recipe to make them. They could let the class try them at break time. That way they would know healthy things can taste great!
Encyclopedia entry on 'healthy diet'	• Lots of factual writing • Organised with sub-headings • Photographs and tables	
Leaflet from a vegan group	• Images of healthy-looking people • Persuasive writing • Links to a website	
Website on the pros and cons of being vegetarian	• Tells you about the issue first • Arguments for with support • Arguments against with support • Organised side by side	
Page in a science textbook on 'digestion'	• Tells you what digestion is • Explains step by step • Labelled diagram	

Take a moment with your group to consider the topic you are working on.
What is it that you want to change?
How will you know that you have been successful?

The issue that my group wants to address is ....

We are concerned that ....

Our goal is to ....

Now consider the sources that you have gathered.
What are their key features? How might they help you reach your goal?

Source	Features	Useful because ...?

Compare your findings with another group. Have they identified any sources of information that would be useful to you? Have they identified any additional features? Have they thought about possible actions that they can take based on their information?

Class discussion

What source has been most useful to you in suggesting appropriate action to take on your issue?

Independent reflection activity

Check your learning goals

If you are sure you have met them and can give a reason why put a '★'.

If you think you have met them put a '☺'.

If you think you are not quite there yet put a '☺'.

2

Starting with evaluation skills: Lesson 2

Evaluation learning objectives

3.1 Evaluating sources

<table>
<tr><td colspan="3">Lesson learning goals</td></tr>
<tr><td colspan="3">These are the goals for this lesson.
You will return to this table at the end of the lesson for the independent reflection activity.</td></tr>
<tr><td>My learning goals
To start to:</td><td>I think</td><td>My teacher/
partner thinks</td></tr>
<tr><td>recognise some strong points about a source</td><td></td><td></td></tr>
<tr><td>recognise some limitations of a source</td><td></td><td></td></tr>
</table>

Prior learning

Remember Zara's topic is 'Keeping healthy'. Her goals are to raise awareness about healthy eating and give her class some new ideas.

Hold a class discussion: Should Zara use the information in this advertisement? Explain your answer.

Starter activity

The topic I am working on today is:

....

Take a moment with your group to reconsider the topic you are working on. Are you still clear on what it is that you want to change? Are you still in agreement about how you will know that you have been successful?

My group is concerned that ....

Our goal is to ....

Main activity

What is the most useful source that you have been able to find?

How will it help you to achieve your goal?

Use the sentence starters below to help you explain your answer.

The most useful source we have found so far is ....

There are several reasons for this; firstly, ...

In addition, ...

....

....

Furthermore, ...

....

Finally, ...

....

However, this source still has limitations.
The first of these is that

....

Also, ...

....

So we will need to find additional sources to help us

....

....

Peer feedback

Show your evaluation to a partner, and ask them to tell you …

Two things that they like about it (write what they tell you here):

⭐ ....

⭐ ....

One thing that you could do better (write what they tell you here):

☄ ....

Independent reflection activity

Check your learning goals

If you are sure you have met them and can give a reason why put a '★'.

If you think you have met them put a '☺'.

If you think you are not quite there yet put a '☺'.

Self-assessment Lessons 1–2

How will I know if I have achieved my learning goals?

Use this activity to reflect on how well you have progressed over the last two lessons.

Tick (✓) 'Achieved' if you are sure you have made good progress with this skill and can give an example.

Tick (✓) 'Not there yet / with help' if you need some further practice so that you can make more progress.

If you tick 'Achieved', then challenge yourself to make further progress in the next section.

If you tick 'Not there yet / with help', there will be the chance to consolidate this skill in future lessons.

Evaluation learning objectives To start to:	Not there yet / with help	Achieved	Example
evaluate sources			

Reflect on your responses in your self-assessment and identify one area for improvement.

One area I want to improve in is:

....

How I will improve:

....

Challenge topic review

Think about the Challenge topic you have been exploring and complete the following statements.

I was surprised to discover/explore that ....

....

I did not know ....

....

I now think ....

....

Developing evaluation skills: Lesson 3

Evaluation learning objectives

3.1 Evaluating sources

3.2 Evaluating arguments

<table>
<tr><td colspan="3">Lesson learning goals</td></tr>
<tr><td colspan="3">These are the goals for this lesson.
You will return to this table at the end of the lesson for the independent reflection activity.</td></tr>
<tr><td>My learning goals
To develop my knowledge and understanding about:</td><td>I think</td><td>My teacher/
partner thinks</td></tr>
<tr><td>how to say what the main viewpoint of a source is</td><td></td><td></td></tr>
<tr><td>how to locate words/phrases from a source that could be useful</td><td></td><td></td></tr>
</table>

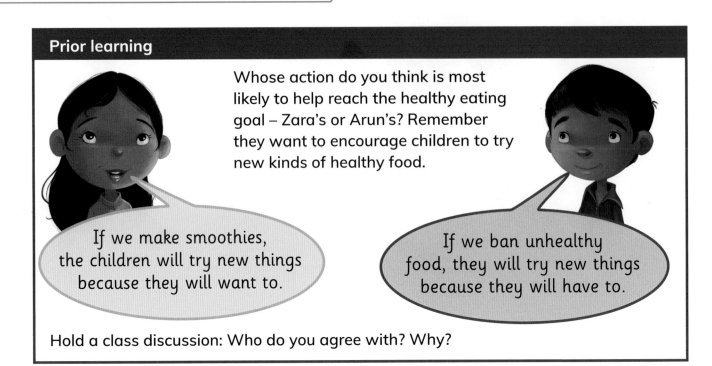

Prior learning

Whose action do you think is most likely to help reach the healthy eating goal – Zara's or Arun's? Remember they want to encourage children to try new kinds of healthy food.

> If we make smoothies, the children will try new things because they will want to.

> If we ban unhealthy food, they will try new things because they will have to.

Hold a class discussion: Who do you agree with? Why?

Starter activity

In Cambridge Global Perspectives, we need to work with facts *and* opinions. We want to persuade people to make a positive change. If we *just* deal in facts, we will struggle to persuade people. If we *just* deal with opinions, people will not see these as a good reason to change. We are more likely to reach our goal if we can use both.

How could we use these sources of information?
The first one has been done for you.

Source	Mainly so that we can get facts	Mainly so that we can get different perspectives
An encyclopedia entry	✓	
A pamphlet from a campaign group with a title like 'Five reasons to take action now!'		✓
A report about school leaving age in different countries		
A page in a geography textbook, e.g. about volcanoes		

Source	Mainly so that we can get facts	Mainly so that we can get different perspectives
An article giving a balanced account of both sides of an issue, e.g. for/against		
A page in a science book, e.g. how the digestive system works		
A newspaper column with a title like 'Why this chaos must stop!'		

Main activity

The topic I am working on today is:

....

Arun has been looking at text on healthy eating – your teacher will give you the report that he has been reading. He has been picking out the main ideas (he highlights these in yellow). He has also been trying to pick out phrases in the report that would help his team meet their goals (he highlights these in green). Your teacher will give you the work he has done so far – can you finish his summary?

Class discussion

1   What would you say the message of the article is?
2   What would you say are the strengths of the source?
3   What would you say are its weaknesses?
4   What is in the article that would help Zara and Arun meet their goal?

Independent reflection activity

Check your learning goals

If you are sure you have met them and can give a reason why put a '★'.

If you think you have met them put a '☺'.

If you think you are not quite there yet put a '☺'.

Developing evaluation skills: Lesson 4

Evaluation learning objectives

3.1 Evaluating sources

3.2 Evaluating arguments

Lesson learning goals		
These are the goals for this lesson. You will return to this table at the end of the lesson for the independent reflection activity.		
My learning goals To develop my knowledge and understanding about:	I think	My teacher/ partner thinks
reasons for choosing a source		
comparing the features of different sources		
comparing what different sources say about a topic		

Prior learning

Can you match the sources below to the person who might find them useful? The first one has been started for you. Tip: each person will need more than one source!

Topic: Healthy eating

Goal: *To raise awareness and get children in her school to try new healthy food.*

Zara ....1........ (there may be more!) ....

Topic: Keeping safe

Goal: *To make sure young children in his community know how to stay safe online.*

Arun ....

Topic: Reduce, reuse, recycle

Goal: *To encourage members of her community to cut down on single-use plastics.*

Sofia ....

1 Magazine article: 'The new super foods'
2 Survey: How many times did you throw a cup away last week?
3 Online article: 'The great Pacific garbage dump'
4 Recipe: Zingy orange, ginger and carrot juice
5 Survey: What computer games do you play?
6 Magazine article: 'Top tips for a plastic-free Halloween'
7 Government leaflet: 'Phishing scams and how to avoid them'
8 Newspaper article: 'Freetown police called in to fight hacker attacks'
9 Survey: How many portions of fruit did you eat yesterday?

Starter activity

Sofia wants her school to take action against a brand of sweet called 'Rabido'.

Read the article 'Health worries over sweet sensation' in the download that your teacher will give you. Use annotations/highlighting (as you did in Lesson 3) to identify:

1 Who wrote the article? (annotate)
2 What is the problem? (annotate)
3 Where is this problem taking place? (annotate)

Extra challenge: What sentences could Sofia use to persuade her school to ban Rabido? (highlight them)

Class discussion

Share your ideas in a class discussion.

Main activity

Sofia has found four more sources on the issue. Your teacher will give these to you.

Compare them using the table provided with the sources (one has been done for you). Give each source a score.

1 = most useful to Sofia, 2 = quite useful, 3 = not so useful, 4 = least useful to Sofia.

Enter your score in the table below.

Source	A	B	C	D
Score				

Which source would be the most useful to Sofia to help her justify her action? Why?

Source .... because ....

....

....

The topic I am working on today is:

....

The issue I want to address is ....

....

The action I want to take is ....

....

This is because ....

....

Class discussion

Be ready to tell the class:

- what issue you are working on
- the action you want to take
- what sources you now have that you think you could use to help justify your action
- how they provide support for your action.

Independent reflection activity

Check your learning goals

If you are sure you have met them and can give a reason why put a '★'.

If you think you have met them put a '☺'.

If you think you are not quite there yet put a '☺'.

Self-assessment Lessons 3–4

How will I know if I have achieved my learning goals?

Use this activity to reflect on how well you have progressed over the last two lessons.

Tick (✓) 'Achieved' if you are sure you have made good progress with this skill and can give an example.

Tick (✓) 'Not there yet / with help' if you need some further practice so that you can make more progress.

If you tick 'Achieved', then challenge yourself to make further progress in the next section.

If you tick 'Not there yet / with help', there will be the chance to consolidate this skill in future lessons.

Continued

Evaluation learning objectives To develop my knowledge and understanding about:	Not there yet / with help	Achieved	Example
evaluating sources			
evaluating arguments			

Reflect on your responses in your self-assessment and identify one area for improvement.

One area I want to improve in is:

....

How I will improve:

....

Challenge topic review

Think about the Challenge topic you have been exploring and complete the following statements.

I was surprised to discover/explore that ....

....

I did not know ....

....

I now think ....

....

5

Getting better at evaluation skills: Lesson 5

Evaluation learning objectives

3.1 Evaluating sources

3.2 Evaluating arguments

Lesson learning goals		
These are the goals for this lesson. You will return to this table at the end of the lesson for the independent reflection activity.		

My learning goals To get better at:	I think	My teacher/ partner thinks
giving my reasons for choosing a source		
comparing the features and viewpoints of different sources		

Prior learning

Zara and her group would like to help solve the problem of plastic pollution in their area by persuading the school to set up a recycling point for plastic.

Which of these sources do you think might be useful in helping them to persuade the school to do this? Tick the two that you think might be most useful and say why.

a   an online advertisement for a brand of mineral water sold in plastic bottles

b   a blog by local residents who are complaining about the litter in the park

c   a newspaper article about supermarkets making customers pay for plastic carrier bags

d   a brochure from a recycling company advertising the services they offer to customers

e   a scientific report about the effects of plastic pollution on wildlife in the oceans

f   an interview on local radio with a politician discussing climate change

Starter activity

The topic I am working on today is:

....

In your group, think of a local problem, and an action you would like to take to help to solve that problem.

Our local problem ....

Our action ....

1   What sources could you use to support your action?

....

2   Which source do you think would be most useful?

....

Class discussion

What makes a source useful when it comes to supporting an action?

Main activity

Find two sources on the local problem that you would like to take action on, or use the sources provided by your teacher. Compare them using this table:

Sources	Source A	Source B
Purpose		
Viewpoint		
Author		
Strengths		
Limitations		

Which source would be the most useful to help you justify your action?

Source .... because ....

....

Class discussion

Report to the class on the source you have chosen, and why.

Independent reflection activity

Check your learning goals

If you are sure you have met them and can give a reason why put a '★'.

If you think you have met them put a '☺'.

If you think you are not quite there yet put a '☺'.

Self-assessment Lesson 5

How will I know if I have achieved my learning goals?

Use this activity to reflect on how well you have progressed over the last lesson.

Tick (✓) 'Achieved' if you are sure you have made good progress with this skill and can give an example.

Tick (✓) 'Not there yet / with help' if you need some further practice so that you can make more progress.

If you tick 'Achieved', then challenge yourself to make further progress in the next section.

If you tick 'Not there yet / with help', there will be the chance to consolidate this skill in future lessons.

Evaluation learning objectives To get better at:	Not there yet / with help	Achieved	Example
evaluating sources			
evaluating arguments			

Continued

Reflect on your responses in your self-assessment and identify one area for improvement.

One area I want to improve in is:

....

How I will improve:

....

Challenge topic review

Think about the Challenge topic you have been exploring and complete the following statements.

I was surprised to discover/explore that ....

....

I did not know ....

....

I now think ....

....

Starting with reflection skills: Lesson 1

Reflection learning objectives

4.3 Personal viewpoints

4.4 Personal learning

Lesson learning goals		
These are the goals for this lesson. You will return to this table at the end of the lesson for the independent reflection activity.		
My learning goals To start to:	I think	My teacher/ partner thinks
talk about what I have learnt and how my ideas have changed		
talk about a skill that I have got better at		

Prior learning
Zara and her group have been finding out about the problem of plastic pollution and what can be done about it.
Work in a group. Your teacher will give each of you a different set of notes that Zara's team made while they were doing their research.

Continued

Look at the notes you are given and write down three important facts about plastic. You should try to find facts that would help to persuade people to do something about plastic pollution.

My top three facts about plastic:

1 ....

2 ....

3 ....

Tell the other members of your group the three facts you have written down and explain why you chose them. Listen to the facts that other members of your group tell you.

Starter activity

These are some of things that members of Zara's group said while they were working on a team project.

OK, Arun, you've been talking for over a minute and Sofia hasn't spoken yet. Let's hear what she's found out.

We agreed to spend 15 minutes finding some sources on this topic. Time's almost up, so is everyone ready?

Our group investigated the topic of disposable plastics. The first thing we did was to find some reliable sources.

OK, so I'll write down that we've decided to investigate single-use plastics and what can be done about them.

Which member of the group played which role?

Facilitator (making sure that everyone takes part) ....

Recorder (keeping notes of what the team does) ....

Reporter (telling the class what the team has done) ....

Timekeeper (checking deadlines are met) ....

Class discussion

1   What other roles can there be in a team?
2   What role do you prefer to have when working in a team, and why?

Main activity

The topic I am working on today is:

....

Look at the teamwork roles in the starter activity and decide what role each person in your group will take for the following task. With the other members of your group, discuss which four facts about plastic you think will have the most powerful impact when you tell other people about them. When you have agreed what those facts are, write them down here:

My group's top four facts about plastic:

1   ....

2   ....

3   ....

4   ....

Now think about the activities that you have just done:

1   What is the most important fact that you have learnt about plastic?

   ....

2   How will this information change the way you think about plastic?

   ....

3   How will this affect what you do in future?

   ....

4   What skills have you used in these activities?

   ....

5   Which of these skills have you got better at?

   ....

6   Which of these skills would you like to improve at?

   ....

Class discussion

1   What skills are important for successful teamwork?
2   How can these skills be improved?

Independent reflection activity

Check your learning goals

If you are sure you have met them and can give a reason why put a '★'.

If you think you have met them put a '☺'.

If you think you are not quite there yet put a '☺'.

Starting with reflection skills: Lesson 2

Reflection learning objectives

4.1 Personal contribution

4.2 Teamwork

Lesson learning goals		
These are the goals for this lesson. You will return to this table at the end of the lesson for the independent reflection activity.		
My learning goals To start to:	I think	My teacher/ partner thinks
talk about what I did as a member of my team		
talk about positive or negative experiences when working as a member of a team		

Prior learning

Zara uses cotton buds or swabs. She recently found this source:

'Many people use cotton buds or swabs to clean their ears or to remove make up. What's wrong with that? The problem is, apart from the cotton tips, most cotton buds are made of plastic, and after just one use we simply throw them away – or, worse still, flush them down the toilet. And where do they end up? Discarded cotton buds join the ever-increasing amount of plastic waste causing damage to our environment ...'

1 Who do you think wrote this?

   a   a medical doctor

   b   an environmental campaigner

   c   an advertiser for a plastics company

   d   a scientist studying life in the sea

2 Why do you think they wrote it?

   a   to report on their research findings

   b   to sell more cotton buds

   c   to advise people to clean their ears

   d   to persuade people to use less plastic

Discuss the following questions with a partner.

1 What action do you think Zara could take after reading this?

2 What other items made of plastic do you used every day?

Starter activity

Zara and her group have made a list of things made of plastic. Apart from the material they are made from, what do you think they all have in common? Which of them do you use most? Number them from 1 to 10, with 1 being the one you use most and 10 the one you use least.

Plastic item	Number (1–10)
shopping bags (e.g. plastic supermarket carrier bags)	
disposable drinks bottles (e.g. plastic water bottles)	
cutlery (e.g. plastic spoons, forks or stirrers)	
takeout food containers (e.g. plastic containers for hot food from a fast food restaurant)	
drinking straws	
sachets containing sauces for food (e.g. ketchup, vinegar or mayonnaise)	
sachets containing cosmetics (e.g. shampoo or liquid soap)	
personal hygiene items (e.g. cotton buds or face wipes)	
eating or drinking utensils (e.g. plastic cups or plates)	
food packaging (e.g. wrappers for sweets or film for wrapping around fresh food and sandwiches)	

Talk to a partner about which of these items you use the most and why.
What could you do to use less plastic?

Class discussion

All the items in the list in the Starter activity are mainly designed to be used just once and then thrown away. They are called single-use or disposable plastics.

1   What happens to these items when people throw them away?
2   What effects does plastic waste have?
3   What can be done to stop creating so much plastic waste?

Main activity

The topic I am working on today is:

....

Zara and her group have been talking about ways in which they could help to reduce the amount of plastic waste.

> What could we do about plastic takeout containers? People use them once and then throw them away.

> I know. The litter they cause on our streets is bad enough, and then they take years to decompose.

> Perhaps we can advise people to cook more food at home, using fresh ingredients?

> Yes, we could put up posters encouraging more home cooking. It's healthier than fast food anyway!

Work in a group. Before you begin this activity, decide what role each member of the team will take. Look at the list of plastic items in the starter activity. With the other members of your group, choose four of them that you would all like to do something about. What action could you take?

Plastic item	Action

Peer feedback

Think about the activity you have just done in your group. For each person in your group, including yourself, think of one way that they helped the group to complete this activity.

Name of group member	Contribution to teamwork

Share your ideas with the others in your group and decide what was the most helpful thing that each person did.

1   What do the other group members think your most helpful contribution was? Write it here:

   ....

2   What was one advantage of doing this activity as a team?

   ....

3   What was one disadvantage?

   ....

Class discussion

1   What are the different ways that each group member can help to make teamwork successful?

2   How can teamwork be improved?

Independent reflection activity

Check your learning goals

If you are sure you have met them and can give a reason why put a '★'.

If you think you have met them put a '☺'.

If you think you are not quite there yet put a '☺'.

Starting with reflection skills: Lesson 3

Reflection learning objectives

4.1 Personal contribution

4.2 Teamwork

4.3 Personal viewpoints

4.4 Personal learning

Lesson learning goals

These are the goals for this lesson.
You will return to this table at the end of the lesson for the independent reflection activity.

My learning goals To start to:	I think	My teacher/ partner thinks
talk about what I did as a member of my team		
talk about positive or negative experiences when working as a member of a team		
talk about what I have learnt and how my ideas have changed		
talk about a skill that I have got better at		

Prior learning

Here are some of the things that Marcus's group said when they reflected on their team project. What skills were they talking about? Write their name in the table under that skill.

Marcus: 'We decided that one of the sources we found wasn't reliable because it wasn't clear who the author was.'

Sofia: 'My most important role was checking that everyone finished their task on time, so the team could achieve its goal.'

Arun: 'The results of our research showed that one of the main causes of plastic pollution is single-use or disposable plastics.'

Zara: 'The question we decided to investigate was 'Is recycling the best solution to the problem of plastic waste?''

	Research	Analysis	Evaluation	Reflection
Name:				

Talk to a partner. Which of these skills do you feel confident in? Which would you like to improve at?

First activity

The topic I am working on today is:

....

Zara and her group have decided to give a presentation to other learners in a school assembly to persuade them to use less plastic in their daily lives. They want to include some slides in their presentation but, as time is limited, they can only show two slides.

Imagine you and your group are in a similar situation to Zara's group. Work with the other group members to plan a presentation about plastic using just two slides. (At this stage, you only need to plan what the slides will show – you can decide what to say about them later.)

Before you begin, think about how to organise the work among the members of your team.

Use A4 paper, or your preferred materials, to design your slides.

Class discussion

1   How did your group organise the work?
2   How did your group make sure that everyone took part?
3   How did your group make sure that the work was finished on time?

Second activity

With a partner, reflect on the teamwork activity that your group has just done.

	I noticed ...	My partner noticed ...
Something good about the way your team worked		
Something that could be improved next time		
Something you learnt about teamwork		
Something you did that helped your team		
Something you could do differently next time		
Some skills that you used during teamwork		

Report back to the class. What was similar about the experiences you and your partner had during the teamwork activity? What was different?

Independent reflection activity

Check your learning goals

If you are sure you have met them and can give a reason why put a '★'.

If you think you have met them put a '☺'.

If you think you are not quite there yet put a '☹'.

Self-assessment Lessons 1–3

How will I know if I have achieved my learning goals?

Use this activity to reflect on how well you have progressed over the last three lessons.

Tick (✓) 'Achieved' if you are sure you have made good progress with this skill and can give an example.

Tick (✓) 'Not there yet / with help' if you need some further practice so that you can make more progress.

If you tick 'Achieved', then challenge yourself to make further progress in the next section.

If you tick 'Not there yet / with help', there will be the chance to consolidate this skill in future lessons.

Reflection learning objectives To start to:	Not there yet / with help	Achieved	Example
reflect on personal contribution			
reflect on teamwork			
reflect on personal viewpoints			
reflect on personal learning			

Continued

Reflect on your responses in your self-assessment and identify one area for improvement.

One area I want to improve in is:

....

How I will improve:

....

Challenge topic review

Think about the Challenge topic you have been exploring and complete the following statements.

I was surprised to discover/explore that ....

....

I did not know ....

....

I now think ....

....

Developing reflection skills: Lesson 4

Reflection learning objectives

4.1 Personal contribution

4.2 Teamwork

Lesson learning goals		
These are the goals for this lesson. You will return to this table at the end of the lesson for the independent reflection activity.		
My learning goals To develop my knowledge and understanding about:	I think	My teacher/ partner thinks
how to talk about what I did as a member of my team		
how to talk about positive or negative experiences when working as a member of a team		

Prior learning

Look at the texts about insects below and match each text with a source. One example has been done for you.

Sources

A Advertisement for a pesticide spray

B Biology textbook

C Newspaper article

D Post on an online nature blog

E Video posted online

Texts

1 According to a recent scientific report, insect numbers are dropping sharply. In some countries, it is estimated that there are 50 percent fewer insects than there were just 15 years ago. | C |

2 Nine out of ten farmers say that Zappit protects their crops by killing 100 percent of insect pests. For best results, get Zappit! | |

3 Has anyone noticed how few butterflies there are this year? Normally the flowers in the nearby park are covered in them during the summer, but this year there are hardly any. | |

4 When I was young, if we made a car journey during the summer, at the end of it we had to clean dead insects off the car windscreen. Now look at this: I have just driven 100 kilometres, and as you can see there is not one dead insect on my windscreen. What is going on? | |

5 Insects are an important part of food chains and food webs. Many other animal species depend on insects as a source of food, without which they could not survive. | |

Talk to a partner.
Which sources do you think give the most reliable information? Why?

Class discussion

1 What do you know about bees?

2 How do bees and other insects affect your lives?

First activity

The topic I am working on today is:

....

Marcus, Sofia, Arun and Zara are working on a team project about bees. They want to raise people's awareness about the importance of bees, and have thought of four questions to do research on. Each of them has made notes from a different source, and now they are going to share information, in order to complete this grid:

Bee project	
What interesting facts are there about bees?	How do bees as pollinators help people?
What else are bees useful for?	Why are bees in danger?

Work in a group. Your teacher will give each of you a different set of notes about bees and a template so that you can complete the grid. Share the information with others in your group by telling them anything from your notes that will help to answer the questions. Write down information that the others tell you in the appropriate boxes. (Tip: you will only have a limited time to do this and you may not need all the information in your notes. Share the information that you think is most important with your group.)

Second activity

Reflect on the previous activity and think about your answers to these questions. Then discuss them with a partner:

1   How did you help your group to complete the task?

    ....

2   Is there anything that you could have done better or differently to help your group complete the task?

    ....

3   Did working as a team make it easier or harder to complete the task? Why?

    ....

4   What have you learnt about teamwork from completing this task?

    ....

Class discussion

1   What is the best way for each member of a team to help the team complete a task?
2   What are the advantages and disadvantages of working as a team?

Independent reflection activity

Check your learning goals

If you are sure you have met them and can give a reason why put a '★'.

If you think you have met them put a '☺'.

If you think you are not quite there yet put a '☺'.

5

Developing reflection skills: Lesson 5

Reflection learning objectives

4.3 Personal viewpoints

4.4 Personal learning

Lesson learning goals		
These are the goals for this lesson. You will return to this table at the end of the lesson for the independent reflection activity.		

My learning goals To develop my knowledge and understanding about:	I think	My teacher/ partner thinks
how to talk about what I have learnt and how my ideas have changed		
how to talk about a skill that I have got better at		

Prior learning

Marcus is reflecting on a teamwork activity he took part in. Read what he says and think about the answers to the questions.

Before my team did some reading on this topic, I used to think that the only good thing about bees is that they make honey. Then one of the members of my team told me that without bees to pollinate them, many of our important crops would fail, and if that happened food would get a lot more expensive in the shops. One of my other team members said that bees are struggling to survive because of the way some farmers are using pesticides. I looked online and found an article that explained how people in cities could help bees by growing more flowering plants. So I suggested to my team that we could reuse some plastic containers to grow flowers in at school and they agreed.

1 What facts has Marcus learnt about bees?
2 How has this changed the way he thinks about bees?
3 What did Marcus contribute to his team?
4 What skills did Marcus use during the teamwork activity?

Talk with a partner. Discuss the answers to the questions.

Starter activity

Marcus, Sofia, Arun and Zara have made a group decision to create a poster to raise other children's awareness of the importance of bees. The school has agreed to print several copies of the poster, which will be displayed in each classroom.

Class discussion

1 What makes a good poster?
2 What information about bees do you think the team should include on their poster?
3 Why do you think they need to include this information?

These are the different tasks that the team decide they will need to do:

Bee poster project			
What?	Who?	How?	When? How long?
1 Find or create a powerful image about bees	Marcus	Do an online search	At the same time as steps (2) and (3) – 15 mins
2 Create a memorable slogan about bees			
3 Find some important facts about bees			
4 Design the layout of the poster			
5 Create the poster using computer graphics			
6 Print copies of the poster in the school office			
7 Put the posters up in classrooms			

The team decide who should do each task, how they should do it, in what order the tasks should be done and how long each task will take.
One example is shown in the table.

4   Why do you think Marcus has been chosen to find or create an image for the poster?

5   What are the other members of the team doing while he does this?

Main activity

The topic I am working on today is:

....

Work in a group. Plan how your group would carry out the bee poster project. Look at the list of tasks to be done and decide:

- Who in your team will do each of the tasks (1–7)?
- How will they do it?
- In what order and for how long will they do it?

Complete the table. Your team has only two lessons in which to finish the project, so try to make sure that everything can be done in that time.

Class discussion

1   What challenges did you face when working as a team to complete the plan, and how did you overcome them?
2   What skills did you use?
3   What skills would you like to get better at?
4   If you were going to do this activity again, how could you do things differently?

Peer feedback

Show your completed team plan to someone from a different group, and ask them to tell you the answers to these questions:

1 According to the plan, is everyone in the team doing their fair share of the work?	YES/NO
2 Have the best people been chosen to do each of the tasks?	YES/NO
3 Has the team chosen the most practical way of completing each of the tasks?	YES/NO
4 Can the project be completed in the time available?	YES/NO

If the answer to any of the questions is 'NO', what changes could you make to the plan?

....

....

Independent reflection activity
Check your learning goals
If you are sure you have met them and can give a reason why put a '★'.
If you think you have met them put a '☺'.
If you think you are not quite there yet put a '☺'.

Developing reflection skills: Lesson 6

Reflection learning objectives

4.1 Personal contribution

4.2 Teamwork

4.3 Personal viewpoints

4.4 Personal learning

Lesson learning goals

These are the goals for this lesson.
You will return to this table at the end of the lesson for the independent reflection activity.

My learning goals To develop my knowledge and understanding about:	I think	My teacher/ partner thinks
how to talk about what I did as a member of my team		
how to talk about positive or negative experiences when working as a member of a team		
how to talk about what I have learnt and how my ideas have changed		
how to talk about a skill that I have got better at		

Prior learning

Arun has been reflecting on a project that his team has completed recently. He writes a personal reflection, which includes a number of different topics. Match the topics to the numbers in the text. An example has been done for you.

Topic	Number(s)	Local/National
a How working as a team helped Arun.		**Personal reflection** (1) Our team decided to give a presentation on bees to the whole school during assembly. (2) My job was to create some slides using images and important information about bees to show during our presentation. I volunteered to do this because I have used a laptop to give a presentation before. (3) The slides were not as good as I wanted them to be because I had to do it in a hurry. (4) This was because one member of our team who was supposed to find important information about bees did not keep to the deadline, (5) so I had to do it. (6) Luckily another member of the team helped me, so we were still able to finish the work in time for the assembly. (7) From this experience I learnt that it would be useful to have someone in the team to check up on what the others are doing and to make sure that everything is completed on time. When it was time to make our presentation in the assembly, I felt very nervous about (8) giving a speech to a large audience, but (9) the other team members helped me to practise my speech and gave me advice on how to speak in public. In the end, our team's presentation was a great success!
b What the team's goal was.	(1)	
c What Arun did to help the team achieve its goal.		
d Something Arun thinks would make teamwork better in future.		
e What Arun thinks of his efforts to help the team.		
f What Arun found challenging about working in a team.		

First activity

Work in a group. Look at the plan for the bee poster project that your team made in Lesson 5. You are going to carry out steps 1–4 of the plan in today's lesson.

Using a sheet of A4 paper, plan and design the layout of your poster.

Second activity

The topic I am working on today is:

....

1   Think about how you worked as a member of a team. Make a note of:

a   One thing that you personally did to help the team achieve its goal.

....

b   One thing that you would do differently in future.

....

2   Think about the way your team worked. Make a note of:

a   One thing your team did that worked well.

....

b   One thing that could be improved to make your teamwork even better next time.

....

3   Think about how your ideas about teamwork have changed over the past three lessons. Complete this sentence:

I used to think ....

....

but now I think ....

....

4   Think about one thing that has changed in the way you do teamwork. Complete this sentence:

In the past, when I worked in a team, I used to ....

....

but now I ....

....

Class discussion

1   What have you learnt about being a member of a team?
2   How can teamwork be improved?

Independent reflection activity
Check your learning goals
If you are sure you have met them and can give a reason why put a '★'.
If you think you have met them put a '☺'.
If you think you are not quite there yet put a '☺'.

Self-assessment Lessons 4–6

How will I know if I have achieved my learning goals?

Use this activity to reflect on how well you have progressed over the last three lessons.

Tick (✓) 'Achieved' if you are sure you have made good progress with this skill and can give an example.

Tick (✓) 'Not there yet / with help' if you need some further practice so that you can make more progress.

If you tick 'Achieved', then challenge yourself to make further progress in the next section.

If you tick 'Not there yet / with help', there will be the chance to consolidate this skill in future lessons.

Reflection learning objectives To start to:	Not there yet / with help	Achieved	Example
personal contribution			
teamwork			
personal viewpoints			
personal learning			

Reflect on your responses in your self-assessment and identify one area for improvement.

One area I want to improve in is:

....

How I will improve:

....

Challenge topic review

Think about the Challenge topic you have been exploring and complete the following statements.

I was surprised to discover/explore that ....

....

I did not know ....

....

I now think ....

....

7

Getting better at reflection skills: Lesson 7

Reflection learning objectives

4.1 Personal contribution

4.2 Teamwork

Lesson learning goals		
These are the goals for this lesson. You will return to this table at the end of the lesson for the independent reflection activity.		
My learning goals **To get better at:**	I think	My teacher/ partner thinks
being clear and talking in a balanced way about what I did as a member of my team		
being clear and talking in a balanced way about positive or negative experiences when working as a member of a team		

Prior learning

Sofia has been reflecting on teamwork and what a good team needs to do to succeed in its goal. Can you help her finish the table?

Good teams always ...	Good teams never ...
have a clear plan	just do things without thinking

Starter activity

Arun, Marcus, Zara and Sofia have been reflecting on their teamwork in their bee project.

Arun has done some things well:

- He explained how he could have improved his contribution.
- He explained what was good about working with his team.
- He explained what was hard about working with his team.

However, he has not reflected on some other aspects of the project:

- He did not really explain why the group decided on the issue.
- He did not explain the goal.
- He did not really explain why they took the action.
- He did not really show that he had thought about different perspectives.
- He did not really explain how he had helped the team.

The table has been filled in for Arun's reflection. How did the others do? Your teacher will give you a download with all of the team's reflections. Read what they have to say and tick (✓) the table where you think they were successful.

	Arun	Marcus	Zara	Sofia
Did they explain why they decided on the issue?				
Did they explain their goal?				
Did they explain why they took the action?				
Did they show that they had thought about different perspectives?				
Did they explain how they helped the team?				
Did they explain how they could have improved their contribution?	✓			
Did they explain what was good about working as a team?	✓			
Did they explain what was hard about working as a team?	✓			

Class discussion

How did you think they did? Discuss your findings with the class.

Main activity

The topic I am working on today is:

....

Arun, Marcus, Zara and Sofia reflected on their teamwork in their bee project.

Now it is your turn. How do you assess your own contribution to your group's action on an issue relating to your topic? Use the sentence starters provided to help you.

1   The issue we worked on was ....

....

2   This issue is important because ....

....

3   Our goal was ....

    ....

4   The action we decided to take was ....

    ....

5   We thought this would be an effective action because ....

    ....

6   My contribution to the team was ....

    ....

7   I could have improved my contribution by ....

    ....

8   Working as a team helped us to ....

    ....

9   Working as a team was challenging because ....

    ....

Class discussion

What would you say are the main advantages and challenges
of working as part of a team?

Independent reflection activity
Check your learning goals
If you are sure you have met them and can give a reason why put a '★'.
If you think you have met them put a '☺'.
If you think you are not quite there yet put a '☺'.

Getting better at reflection skills: Lesson 8

Reflection learning objectives

4.3 Personal viewpoints

4.4 Personal learning

Lesson learning goals		
These are the goals for this lesson. You will return to this table at the end of the lesson for the independent reflection activity.		
My learning goals To get better at:	I think	My teacher/ partner thinks
talking about how new information or the ideas of others have changed the way I think about a topic		
talking about what skills I have got better at and how		

Prior learning

Marcus, Sofia, Arun and Zara created a poster about the importance of bees.

1 Whose ideas did they want to change?
2 What ideas did they want to change?
3 What was their goal?
4 What skills do you think they developed?

Note your ideas ready for a class discussion.

Starter activity

Marcus, Sofia, Arun and Zara have been developing their reflections. They have been asked to include how their thoughts and behaviour changed in the project. They were also asked to write about how the project helped them develop their skills. Your teacher will give you a download in which they have written their thoughts.

Evaluate their reflections in the table below.

1 If you are sure they have explained their ideas well and given a reason why, put a '★' in that row of the table.
2 If you think they have met them, but maybe the reason is less clear, put a '☺'.
3 If you think they are not quite there yet, put a '☺'.
4 If they have missed this out altogether, put 'N/A'.

How well have they:	Marcus	Sofia	Arun	Zara
explained how their thoughts on the issue have developed?				
explained how their own behaviour has changed?				
explained how their own skills have changed?				
explained how others' behaviour has changed?				
explained connections between what they thought and what they did?				

Main activity

The topic I am working on today is:

....

1 Either:

   a   Write your own reflection how your thoughts and behaviour and skills have developed.

   Or

   b   Imagine that you are Marcus, Sofia, Arun or Zara. Write a better reflection on how your thoughts, behaviour and skills have developed during the project.

Make sure that you:	
1 Explain how your thoughts on the issue have developed.	Before, I used to think .... I now realise that .... This is because ....
2 Explain how your own behaviour has changed.	Before, I used to .... However, now I .... This is because I now know that ....

Make sure that you:	
3 Explain how your own skills have changed.	Before, I used to not (be able to / be so good at) .... However, now (I can / I have improved) .... This is because I needed to ....
4 Explain how others' behaviour has changed.	Before, I noticed that .... used to .... However, now I notice that they .... This is because we ....
5 Explain connections between what you thought and what you did.	The reason that we/I took the decision to .... was because .... At first, we .... This was because ....

Make sure that you:	
5 Explain connections between what you thought and what you did.	Then we .... because it was important to .... Finally, we/I made sure that .... This was because ....

Peer feedback

Show your reflection to your partner and ask them to tell you ...

Two things that they like about your evaluation (write what they tell you here):

One thing that you could do better (write what they tell you here):

 ....

Independent reflection activity
Check your learning goals
If you are sure you have met them and can give a reason why put a '★'.
If you think you have met them put a '☺'.
If you think you are not quite there yet put a '☺'.

9

Getting better at reflection skills: Lesson 9

Reflection learning objectives

4.1 Personal contribution

4.2 Teamwork

4.3 Personal viewpoints

4.4 Personal learning

Lesson learning goals

These are the goals for this lesson.
You will return to this table at the end of the lesson for the independent reflection activity.

My learning goals To get better at:	I think	My teacher/ partner thinks
finding ways in which I can help my team		
understanding some of the benefits and challenges of working together as a team		
understanding how new information or the ideas of others have changed the way people think about a topic		
recognising ways to improve my personal skills		

Prior learning

Think about an action that you completed as part of a team recently.

1 What was the activity?
2 What was your role?
3 How did working as part of a team help you?
4 What was your team's goal?
5 What did you do to help your team achieve its goal?
6 What do you think could have made your team work (even) better?
7 What were the challenges you found about working in a team?

Prepare your answers for a class discussion.

Starter activity

Zara has been reflecting on an action she took last year. She has come up with some of the challenges she and her group faced with some ways to overcome them. Can you match them up? The first one has been done for you.

The challenge we faced ...	Ways to overcome the issue this time ...
We did not know whether or not we had achieved our goal.	Conduct a survey to find out things that the school is doing well, and what needs to be improved before taking action.
We wasted time taking action on something that was not really a problem in our school.	Have a clear action plan that sets out the actions and who is responsible for each of them.
We all worked on some of the tasks, and it was hard because we had different ideas. At the same time some things just did not get done.	Make sure you know before you start how you will monitor and evaluate your actions.
We could not do our presentation in front of the whole school because it was assessment week and there was no assembly.	Have a display board with a clear plan of action on it: include dates of upcoming events and what the team's goals are.
Other children did not know about what we were doing.	Set out a clear timetable of action that takes account of different factors.
Children had habits they did not want to break.	Give clear examples from partner schools about the benefits of the action.

Main activity part 1

Read Arun's reflection on a project he did with his team in two years ago.

Our team decided to give a presentation on healthy eating to the class because it was part of our topic. My job was to make a list of healthy foods. I said that I would do this because I had already done it for homework. My list did not go in to the presentation slides. We mainly worked on our own and the slides were Zara's job. I had a long list of healthy foods and other children in the class knew about them too. We all knew healthy foods are important.

Class discussion

If you were to meet Arun, what suggestions would you make to him about how he could have improved his group action?

1   How could he have improved the things he did and how he helped his team?
2   How could he have made more of the benefits of working together as a team and overcome some of the challenges?
3   How might he have used new information or the ideas of others to develop the way he thought about the topic?
4   How could he have made more of the opportunities to improve his skills?

Main activity part 2

Arun has reflected on the actions he took to promote healthy eating and we have discussed this as a class in the class discussion. Now it is your turn.

The topic I am working on today is:

....

Either:

1   comment constructively on Arun's approach to teamwork in their project 'Action on healthy eating'.

Or

2   comment constructively on a partner's approach to teamwork in a project you took part in. Did their approach to teamwork help you to make a positive change? How could they have done even better?

Use the sentence starters below to help you.

a   Well done for ....

b   I like the way you ....

c   Next time, you could try ....

d   This would help you to ....

e   To improve your teamwork, you could try ....

f   To develop the way you think about an issue, next time you could consider

....

g   To make more of the opportunities to improve your skills, next time you could try

....

Independent reflection activity

Check your learning goals

If you are sure you have met them and can give a reason why put a '★'.

If you think you have met them put a '☺'.

If you think you are not quite there yet put a '☹'.

Self-assessment Lessons 7–9

How will I know if I have achieved my learning goals?

Use this activity to reflect on how well you have progressed over the last three lessons.

Tick (✓) 'Achieved' if you are sure you have made good progress with this skill and can give an example.

Tick (✓) 'Not there yet / with help' if you need some further practice so that you can make more progress.

If you tick 'Achieved', then challenge yourself to make further progress in the next section.

If you tick 'Not there yet / with help', there will be the chance to consolidate this skill in future lessons.

Reflection learning objectives To get better at:	Not there yet / with help	Achieved	Example
reflecting on personal contribution			
reflecting on teamwork			
reflecting on personal viewpoints			
reflecting on personal learning			

Continued

Reflect on your responses in your self-assessment and identify one area for improvement.

One area I want to improve in is:

....

How I will improve:

....

Challenge topic review

Think about the Challenge topic you have been exploring and complete the following statements.

I was surprised to discover/explore that ....

....

I did not know ....

....

I now think ....

....

Starting with collaboration skills: Lesson 1

Collaboration learning objectives

5.1 Cooperation and interdependence

5.2 Engaging in teamwork

Lesson learning goals		
These are the goals for this lesson. You will return to this table at the end of the lesson for the independent reflection activity.		
My learning goals To start to:	I think	My teacher/ partner thinks
work with others to plan a task		
work well with others to solve a problem		

Prior learning

Marcus is reflecting on how he has changed as a result of an investigation his group carried out into the problem of pollution. Read the text in the download that your teacher gives you. Then highlight or underline the part of the text that matches each of the headings below and write the heading number in the left-hand column next to it. One has been done for you.

1   What he used to think about the problem.

2   What he used to do.

3   What he learnt.

4   What he thinks about the problem now.

5   What he does differently now.

Talk with a partner. What else could Marcus do to help solve the problem of plastic pollution?

Starter activity

Marcus and his group want to raise awareness about the problem of plastic pollution at their school. Each member of the group makes a suggestion about how they could do this:

Why don't we display some posters in the entrance? Then everyone will see them as they come to school.

Even better, supposing we created a stall in the entrance, so we can talk to other learners about the problem?

And we could ask learners to complete a questionnaire, and reward them with stickers if they answer our questions.

Yes, then we could also use a table to display some of the things we have made from plastic bottles.

In order to prepare their stall, Marcus's group list the tasks they must do.
Can you think of anything to add to the list?

1   Make posters with information about plastic pollution.
2   Find and decorate a table to make an attractive stall.
3   Reuse plastic bottles to make pen holders and plant pots.
4   Make a questionnaire about plastic pollution.
5   Make stickers with messages about plastic pollution.

6   Other..

Class discussion

1   Which of the tasks are likely to take more time to complete and why?
2   What skills or knowledge are needed to complete each task successfully?
3   How can the tasks be divided fairly between the four members of Marcus's group?

Main activity

The topic I am working on today is:

....

This is the plan showing how Marcus's group have decided to divide up the work.
The group has 90 minutes in which to prepare their stall.

Task	Who?	How long?	When?
1 Make posters with information about plastic pollution.	Sofia	45 minutes	Before tasks 4 and 5
2 Find and decorate a table to make an attractive stall.	Arun	30 minutes	Before tasks 4 and 5
3 Reuse plastic bottles to make pen holders and plant pots.	Zara	45 minutes	Before tasks 4 and 5
4 Make a questionnaire about plastic pollution for learners.	Arun, Zara and Sofia	30 minutes	After tasks 1–3
5 Make stickers with messages about plastic pollution.	Arun, Zara, Sofia and Marcus	10 minutes	After task 4
6 Prepare some slides to make a presentation on a laptop computer.	Marcus	60 minutes	While others do tasks 1–4

Do you think they have succeeded in dividing up the work fairly between them?

Do you think they have given themselves enough time to complete each task?

Revise the plan, making any changes you think necessary, below.
Use the names of the people in your group when completing the 'Who?' column, bearing in mind the skills and knowledge they have.

Task	Who?	How long?	When?
1 Make posters with information about plastic pollution.			
2 Find and decorate a table to make an attractive stall.			
3 Reuse plastic bottles to make pen holders and plant pots.			
4 Make a questionnaire about plastic pollution for learners.			

Task	Who?	How long?	When?
5 Make stickers with messages about plastic pollution.			
6 Prepare some slides to make a presentation on a laptop computer.			

Class discussion

What changes have you made to the original plan? Why?

Independent reflection activity

Check your learning goals

If you are sure you have met them and can give a reason why put a '★'.

If you think you have met them put a '☺'.

If you think you are not quite there yet put a '☺'.

2

Starting with collaboration skills: Lesson 2

Collaboration learning objectives

5.1 Cooperation and interdependence

5.2 Engaging in teamwork

Lesson learning goals		
These are the goals for this lesson. You will return to this table at the end of the lesson for the independent reflection activity.		
My learning goals To start to:	I think	My teacher/ partner thinks
work with others to plan a task		
work well with others to solve a problem		

Prior learning

Arun is talking about a problem that his group had while they were carrying out a teamwork activity:

> Everyone except Marcus had already agreed to do one of the tasks on their own, but no one wanted to write the questionnaire or make the stickers. Zara tried to get Marcus to do one of these tasks, but he refused. When Sofia asked him what he wanted to do, he said that he wanted to make some slides about plastic pollution to show on a laptop as part of our stall. This was not on our list of tasks, but Sofia said that it would make our stall look more attractive, so we agreed to let Marcus do it. We still had not found anyone to make the questionnaire or the stickers, so I suggested that all of us should work together to do these tasks. The others agreed, but Marcus still refused! Then Zara pointed out that it was unfair because everyone else was doing three tasks, but he was only doing one. He finally agreed to help the rest of us make the stickers.

Which member of Arun's group uses the following collaboration skills?

1 .... encourages other team members to take part.

2 .... introduces helpful ideas.

3 .... is open to new ideas.

4 .... helps to resolve conflicts.

Talk to a partner. Which of these skills do you think is the most important?

Starter activity

Work in a group. Imagine that your group is going to create a stall to raise other learners' awareness about an **issue**. Try to avoid choosing plastic pollution as your issue, as you have already looked at this topic in Lesson 1!

The topic I am working on today is:

....

Our issue is ....

What tasks will your group need to do to prepare your stall?
Make a list in the Task column on the left.

Task	Who?	How long?	When?
1			
2			
3			
4			
5			
6			

Main activity

Imagine that you have 90 minutes to finish preparing everything for your stall, which has to be in place by tomorrow morning. Working in your group, complete the rest of the table above by deciding:

1   Which group member(s) will do each task so that the work is divided up fairly.

2   How long each task should take.

3   The order in which each task will be completed.

Report back to the class on your planning process.

Class discussion

1   What roles did each of your group members have while doing these activities?

2   How successful do you think your planning has been? How could it be improved?

3   Did your group have any disagreements? If so, how did you resolve them?

Peer feedback

Talk to a partner from a different group about what you did in this lesson.
Tell your partner about the following:

1 A problem in your group that you helped to solve and how.

2 A helpful idea that you came up with.

3 An idea that another member of the group suggested, and which you agreed to.

Ask your partner to tell you two ways that you collaborated well in your group
(write what they were here):

★ ....

★ ....

Ask them to tell you one way that you could improve your collaboration skills
(write what they tell you here):

 ....

Independent reflection activity

Check your learning goals

If you are sure you have met them and can give a reason why put a '★'.

If you think you have met them put a '☺'.

If you think you are not quite there yet put a '☺'.

Self-assessment Lessons 1–2

How will I know if I have achieved my learning goals?

Use this activity to reflect on how well you have progressed over the
last two lessons.

Tick (✓) 'Achieved' if you are sure you have made good progress with
this skill and can give an example.

Tick (✓) 'Not there yet / with help' if you need some further practice
so that you can make more progress.

Continued

If you tick 'Achieved', then challenge yourself to make further progress in the next section.

If you tick 'Not there yet / with help', there will be the chance to consolidate this skill in future lessons.

Collaboration learning objectives To start to:	Not there yet / with help	Achieved	Example
develop cooperation and interdependence			
engage in teamwork			

Reflect on your responses in your self-assessment and identify one area for improvement.

One area I want to improve in is:

....

How I will improve:

....

Challenge topic review

Think about the Challenge topic you have been exploring and complete the following statements.

I was surprised to discover/explore that ....

....

I did not know ....

....

I now think ....

....

Developing collaboration skills: Lesson 3

Collaboration learning objectives

5.1 Cooperation and interdependence

Lesson learning goals		
These are the goals for this lesson. You will return to this table at the end of the lesson for the independent reflection activity.		
My learning goals To develop my knowledge and understanding about:	I think	My teacher/ partner thinks
how to plan a task to achieve a shared outcome		

Prior learning

I was cloakroom monitor with Sofia. We checked our class kept it tidy for a week. Everyone found their kit!

Hold a class discussion.

1 What do you think the problem was?

2 What was the outcome?

3 What was Arun's task?

4 Who helped him?

5 What can Arun feel proud about?

6 When have you worked with someone to achieve something that you felt proud of?

7 Who helped you?

8 What did you do?

9 What was the outcome?

Starter activity

Can you complete the eight flowcharts? The first one has been done for you.

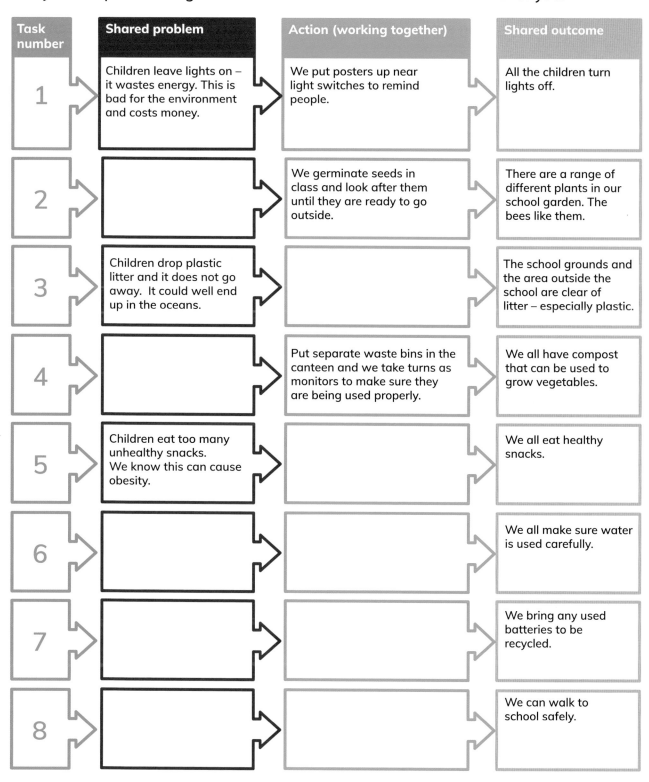

Task number	Shared problem	Action (working together)	Shared outcome
1	Children leave lights on – it wastes energy. This is bad for the environment and costs money.	We put posters up near light switches to remind people.	All the children turn lights off.
2		We germinate seeds in class and look after them until they are ready to go outside.	There are a range of different plants in our school garden. The bees like them.
3	Children drop plastic litter and it does not go away. It could well end up in the oceans.		The school grounds and the area outside the school are clear of litter – especially plastic.
4		Put separate waste bins in the canteen and we take turns as monitors to make sure they are being used properly.	We all have compost that can be used to grow vegetables.
5	Children eat too many unhealthy snacks. We know this can cause obesity.		We all eat healthy snacks.
6			We all make sure water is used carefully.
7			We bring any used batteries to be recycled.
8			We can walk to school safely.

Main activity

Choose a topic to work on from the list below.

Keeping healthy	Keeping safe	Education for all	Sport for all	Understanding each other
Responsible technology	Reduce reuse recycle	Caring for our water	Healthy eating	Sustainable transport
Sustainable food	A fairer world	Respect for young and old	Helping biodiversity	Other ....

The topic I am working on today is:

....

Now complete the flowchart below.

Step 1:   In your group, identify three shared problems associated with your topic.
Record your ideas in the left-hand column of the flowchart.

Step 2:   For each one, decide what the outcome should be.
Record your ideas in the right-hand column of the flowchart.

Step 3:   Decide what action you could take together to get to the outcome.
Record your ideas in the middle column of the flowchart.

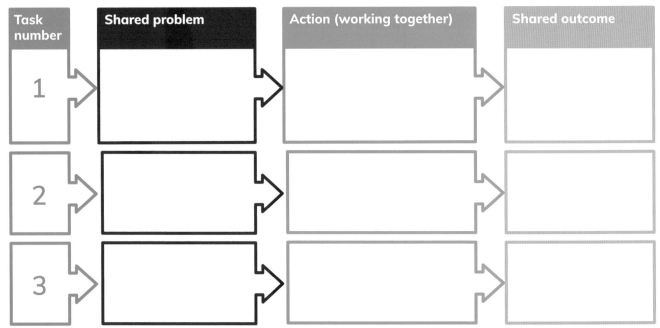

Which action do you might go with you think at this stage if you only have time to take one action? You do not need to make a final decision right now, but here are some things to think about:

- Is it an important problem that needs action to be taken on?
- Will the action change the way people behave?
- Is the outcome realistic?
- Will you be able to work together as a team as part of your action?
- Will you need outside help – and is that help available?

The task that we are prioritising at this stage is ....

This is because, firstly, ...

In addition, ...

Furthermore, ...

Finally, ...

Be ready to report back to the class.

Class discussion

When listening to the other groups, be ready to offer constructive suggestions:

1   Have they identified an important problem that needs action to be taken on?
2   In what way(s) could their action change the way people behave? How could they improve?
3   Is the outcome realistic? Can they measure their success?
4   Will they be able to work together as a team as part of their action? Have they identified how they might divide this up?
5   Will they need outside help – and is that help available? Have you got any suggestions for who they could approach? Or could they do it all by themselves?

Share your ideas with others in the class.

Independent reflection activity

Check your learning goals

If you are sure you have met them and can give a reason why put a '★'.

If you think you have met them put a '☺'.

If you think you are not quite there yet put a '☺'.

Developing collaboration skills: Lesson 4

Collaboration learning objectives

5.2 Engaging in teamwork

Lesson learning goals

These are the goals for this lesson.
You will return to this table at the end of the lesson for the independent reflection activity.

My learning goals To develop my knowledge and understanding about:	I think	My teacher/ partner thinks
introducing useful ideas that help to achieve a shared outcome		
working positively to solve a problem faced by the team		

Prior learning

Your challenge is to make a tower out of **recycled** paper that will support
a weight of 100 g for 30 seconds. Your team will have only 10 cm of tape to use.
Based on what you know already about building and working in groups,
how should your group do this?

Use these sentence starters to help you:

1   Firstly, we will ....

    At this stage, the tasks include: ....

    ....

2   Then, ...

    At this stage, the tasks include: ....

    ....

3   The next step will be to ....

    At this stage, it will be important to ....

    ....

4   After that we will ....

    Each member of the group will need to make sure that ....

    ....

5   Finally ....

    Each member of the group can now ....

Starter activity

Make the tower following the instructions that your teacher will give you.

Then evaluate: how was the tower challenge for you? Complete these sentences:

1 At first, I thought that .... would be a good idea.

2 I later found out that ....

3 A positive contribution I made to the group was ....

4 One good thing about working in a group was that ....

5 One challenge of working in a group was ....

6 One way I could have improved my contribution to the group would have been to

   ....

7 If I were to do the activity again, I would ....

Main activity

The topic I am working on today is:

....

Arun and Zara have been coming up with ideas for ways to encourage children to turn off lights.

They have organised their ideas into a table.

The outcome we want is children turning lights off.

Our suggested actions are:

What? (suggested action)	When?	Where?	Who?	Why?
Give out stickers	When children are leaving their classes, e.g. to go to break	In corridors	Our group giving them to Stage 1 and 2 children.	To encourage them to get into good habits when they are young.
Put up posters	At the start of term	Near switches	Our group to design/make some examples then teach younger children.	To act as a reminder. Encourage responsibility.
Put on an assembly	Whole school assembly	Main hall	Our group performing to the whole school and parents.	Make a big dramatic impact to the whole school.
Make T-shirts	Evenings/weekends	At home	Our group and parents / carers / older siblings who can help.	To advertise the save energy message. Good for the assembly.

Either:

1   Come up with further actions that your group thinks could help Arun and Zara meet their goal.

Or:

2   Come up with actions that you think could help your group meet their goal.

The outcome we want is ....

Our suggested actions are:

What?	When?	Where?	Who?	Why?

Peer feedback

Work with a partner to find out how you showed collaboration skills this lesson.

Ask them to what extent, from their perspective:

- you worked positively with others
- you helped to resolve any disagreements
- you encouraged others to join in
- you made positive suggestions
- you were open to other group members' ideas.

Ask them to tell you two things you did well (write what they were here):

⭐ ....

⭐ ....

One thing that you could do better (write what they tell you here):

☄ ....

Independent reflection activity

Check your learning goals

If you are sure you have met them and can give a reason why put a '★'.

If you think you have met them put a '☺'.

If you think you are not quite there yet put a '☹'.

Self-assessment Lessons 3–4

How will I know if I have achieved my learning goals?

Use this activity to reflect on how well you have progressed over the last two lessons.

Tick (✓) 'Achieved' if you are sure you have made good progress with this skill and can give an example.

Tick (✓) 'Not there yet / with help' if you need some further practice so that you can make more progress.

If you tick 'Achieved', then challenge yourself to make further progress in the next section.

If you tick 'Not there yet / with help', there will be the chance to consolidate this skill in future lessons.

Collaboration learning objectives To develop my knowledge and understanding about:	Not there yet / with help	Achieved	Example
cooperation and interdependence			
engaging in teamwork			

Continued

Reflect on your responses in your self-assessment and identify one area for improvement.

One area I want to improve in is:

....

How I will improve:

....

Challenge topic review

Think about the Challenge topic you have been exploring and complete the following statements.

I was surprised to discover/explore that ....

....

I did not know ....

....

I now think ....

....

5

Getting better at collaboration skills: Lesson 5

Collaboration learning objectives

5.1 Cooperation and interdependence

5.2 Engaging in teamwork

Lesson learning goals		
These are the goals for this lesson. You will return to this table at the end of the lesson for the independent reflection activity.		
My learning goals To get better at:	I think	My teacher/ partner thinks
working with others to plan a task, deciding how long it will take to complete		
working independently on tasks that help to achieve a team goal		

Based on your experiences of teamwork (including in Lesson 4) how would you answer these questions?

1 A good team member always	2 A good team always ....
3 A good team member never	4 A good team never ....

Discuss your answers with the class.

Starter activity

Based on your experiences (including in Lesson 4), how would you evaluate your own approach to teamwork. Tick (✓) the response that you think best matches your approach.

1 I am good at suggesting helpful ideas to my team:

Always	Most of the time	Sometimes	Rarely	Never

2 I respond positively to other people's suggestions:

Always	Most of the time	Sometimes	Rarely	Never

3 If my team has a disagreement, I am good at helping them resolve it.

Always	Most of the time	Sometimes	Rarely	Never

Based on your experiences in Lesson 4, how would you evaluate
your team's performance. Tick (✓) the response that you think best matches
your group's approach.

1   Our team shared the work fairly.

Strongly agree	Agree	Neither agree nor disagree	Disagree	Strongly disagree

2   Our team made sure the members could develop their skills.

Strongly agree	Agree	Neither agree nor disagree	Disagree	Strongly disagree

3   We reached our goal.

Strongly agree	Agree	Neither agree nor disagree	Disagree	Strongly disagree

Based on your **evaluation**, complete these four sentences:

1   To be an even better team member, next time I will aim to ....

   ....

2   This is because ....

   ....

3   To be an even better team, next time we must aim to ....

   ....

4   This is because ....

   ....

Main activity

The topic I am working on today is:

....

The issue that my group wants to address is ....

My group's goal is to ....

You are going to use the table below to formulate your action plan.

Break down your main goal into a series of steps. Write them here.	Write down the name (or initials) of the group member responsible here.	Think about what order you will need to do things in. Think about what actions depend on others being completed first.	Think about what you will need to complete the task successfully. Make lists here.	This is where you record how you are doing: Red – not yet done. Yellow – partially complete. Green – completed.
Action	Who?	By when?	Resources needed?	Status?
				R / Y / G
				R / Y / G
				R / Y / G
				R / Y / G
				R / Y / G

Based on your experiences working towards this goal, how would you evaluate your own approach to teamwork. Tick (✓) the response that you think best matches your approach.

1   I was good at suggesting helpful ideas to my team:

Always	Most of the time	Sometimes	Rarely	Never

2   I responded positively to other people's suggestions:

Always	Most of the time	Sometimes	Rarely	Never

3   If my team had a disagreement, I was good at helping them resolve it.

Always	Most of the time	Sometimes	Rarely	Never

Based on your experiences working towards this goal, how would you evaluate your team's performance. Tick (✓) the response that you think best matches your group's approach.

1   Our team shared the work fairly.

Strongly agree	Agree	Neither agree nor disagree	Disagree	Strongly disagree

2   Our team made sure the members could develop their skills.

Strongly agree	Agree	Neither agree nor disagree	Disagree	Strongly disagree

3   We reached our goal.

Strongly agree	Agree	Neither agree nor disagree	Disagree	Strongly disagree

Class discussion

How have your collaboration skills improved?

Independent reflection activity

Check your learning goals

If you are sure you have met them and can give a reason why put a '★'.

If you think you have met them put a '☺'.

If you think you are not quite there yet put a '☺'.

Self-assessment Lesson 5

How will I know if I have achieved my learning goals?

Use this activity to reflect on how well you have progressed over the last lesson.

Tick (✓) 'Achieved' if you are sure you have made good progress with this skill and can give an example.

Tick (✓) 'Not there yet / with help' if you need some further practice so that you can make more progress.

If you tick 'Achieved', then challenge yourself to make further progress in the next section.

If you tick 'Not there yet / with help', there will be the chance to consolidate this skill in future lessons.

Continued

Collaboration learning objectives To get better at:	Not there yet / with help	Achieved	Example
cooperation and interdependence			
engaging in teamwork			

Reflect on your responses in your self-assessment and identify one area for improvement.

One area I want to improve in is:

....

How I will improve:

....

Challenge topic review

Think about the Challenge topic you have been exploring and complete the following statements.

I was surprised to discover/explore that ....

....

I did not know ....

....

I now think ....

....

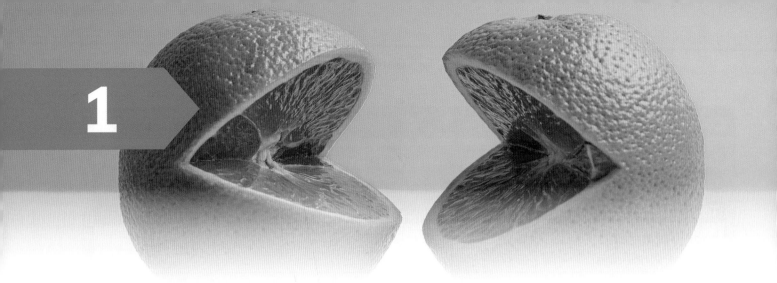

1

Starting with communication skills: Lesson 1

Communication learning objectives

6.1 Communicating information

6.2 Listening and responding

Lesson learning goals
These are the goals for this lesson. You will return to this table at the end of the lesson for the independent reflection activity.

My learning goals To start to:	I think	My teacher/ partner thinks
tell other people about a topic so that they can understand it better		
listen to what someone tells me about a topic and respond by asking questions		

Prior learning		
Here are some of the things that Marcus said during a discussion with his teammates about how they should carry out a team project. Find the different things he says to help his team **collaborate** and achieve their goal.		
How Marcus helps his team to collaborate	**Number**	
a Accepts new ideas from other team members		**Personal reflection** **(1)** Writing the report has to be a team effort, so why don't we wait until we have finished all the other things we are going to do for our team project and then write it together? Then we will also be able to write about what went well and what didn not go so well. **(2)** We have each got a different task to complete first and each of us is going to do something that we are really good at. **(3)** I know Sofia thinks that it is a bit unfair because her task is going to take longer than anyone else's, so anyone who finishes their task before she does, you should try to help her. **(4)** Arun says he can print the poster at home and I think that is a great idea because then we don't have to ask the school to print it for us. **(5)** I am really looking forward to working with everyone to make our team project a success.
b Suggests a helpful idea or solution		
c Cooperates positively with others in his team		
d Helps to resolve a conflict		
e Encourages others to take part		

Talk with a partner.

Which of the things that Marcus says do you think is the most helpful? Why?

Starter activity

Every year, Zara's school raises money to help a **local** organisation. This year, a nearby zoo has asked the school to support them. Zara and her team have carried out some **research** and are going to decide whether or not they think raising money to support the zoo is a good idea.

Class discussion

1 What are some arguments in favour of keeping animals in zoos?
2 What are some arguments against?

Main activity

The topic I am working on today is:

....

Work in a group. Your teacher will give each of you a **source** with some arguments for and against zoos, and a chart for you to make notes. Tell the rest of the group about the arguments in your source. Listen to the arguments that the other group members tell you about from their sources. Make notes in the chart that your teacher gives you. Ask other members of the group questions if anything is not clear to you.

Class discussion

1 What do you think is the strongest argument in favour of zoos? Why?
2 What is the strongest argument against zoos and why?

Now that you have read and listened to arguments for and against zoos, what would you advise Zara and her team to do? Should they raise money to support the zoo, or not?

....

Independent reflection activity

Check your learning goals

If you are sure you have met them and can give a reason why put a '★'.

If you think you have met them put a '☺'.

If you think you are not quite there yet put a '☺'.

Starting with communication skills: Lesson 2

Communication learning objectives

6.1 Communicating information

6.2 Listening and responding

Lesson learning goals		
These are the goals for this lesson. You will return to this table at the end of the lesson for the independent reflection activity.		
My learning goals To start to:	I think	My teacher/ partner thinks
tell other people about a topic so that they can understand it better		
listen to what someone tells me about a topic and respond by asking questions		

Prior learning

Arun has been reading this source about cycling in cities.

Cycling is a much cleaner and more efficient method of moving around a city than using non-electric cars or other vehicles as it does not release toxic fumes into the atmosphere and does not cause congestion. However, there are risks for the cyclist. For example, if there are no special lanes to keep them away from other traffic, cyclists can become invisible to motorists, increasing the likelihood of accidents. Furthermore, in these situations, cyclists are also more likely to be exposed to harmful gases from other vehicles, which can damage their health. On the other hand, cycling can improve a cyclist's physical fitness and help to prevent long-term health problems such as heart disease and obesity.

Arun analyses the source, finding arguments for and against, and ideas or examples that are used to support the arguments. Read the source and complete the table below:

	Arguments	Supporting ideas/ examples
For cycling in cities		
Against cycling in cities		

Talk with a partner. Discuss other arguments for or against cycling in cities that you can think of

Starter activity

The topic I am working on today is:

....

Look at the notes you made in Lesson 1 about the arguments for and against zoos.

In your group, decide whether you want to argue for zoos, or against them. Note down the three arguments that you think will be most effective in persuading others to agree with you.

We are going to argue for/against (please choose one) zoos. The three most effective arguments are:

1 ....

2 ....

3 ....

Class discussion

1 What is the best way of organising information when presenting an argument?
2 What can you do to make your argument more persuasive when presenting it to an audience?

Main activity

In your group, make a plan of how you will present your argument. Use the template that your teacher gives you.

Peer feedback

Show your completed team plan to someone from a different
group and ask them to tell you the answers to these questions:

1 Has the issue been clearly defined in the introduction?   YES/NO

2 Is each of the arguments clearly stated?   YES/NO

3 Is each of the arguments supported by adding more detail or giving
   examples?   YES/NO

4 Is there a clear conclusion to the argument?   YES/NO

If the answer to any of the questions is 'NO', make changes to the plan.

Class discussion

Present your argument to the class. Respond to questions that others ask.
Listen to other groups present their argument for or against zoos to the class.
Ask questions if anything is unclear.

Independent reflection activity

Check your learning goals

If you are sure you have met them and can give a reason why put a '★'.

If you think you have met them put a '☺'.

If you think you are not quite there yet put a '☺'.

Self-assessment Lessons 1–2

How will I know if I have achieved my learning goals?

Use this activity to reflect on how well you have progressed over the
last two lessons.

Tick (✓) 'Achieved' if you are sure you have made good progress with
this skill and can give an example.

Tick (✓) 'Not there yet / with help' if you need some further practice
so that you can make more progress.

Continued

If you tick 'Achieved', then challenge yourself to make further progress in the next section.

If you tick 'Not there yet / with help', there will be the chance to consolidate this skill in future lessons.

Communication learning objectives To start to:	Not there yet / with help	Achieved	Example
communicate information			
listen and respond			

Reflect on your responses in your self-assessment and identify one area for improvement.

One area I want to improve in is:

....

How I will improve:

....

Challenge topic review

Think about the Challenge topic you have been exploring and complete the following statements.

I was surprised to discover/explore that ....

....

I did not know ....

....

I now think ....

....

Developing communication skills: Lesson 3

Communication learning objectives

6.1 Communicating information

<table>
<tr><td colspan="3">Lesson learning goals</td></tr>
<tr><td colspan="3">These are the goals for this lesson.
You will return to this table at the end of the lesson for the independent reflection activity.</td></tr>
<tr><th>My learning goals
To develop my knowledge and understanding about:</th><th>I think</th><th>My teacher/
partner thinks</th></tr>
<tr><td>how to present information on a topic using a clear structure</td><td></td><td></td></tr>
<tr><td>how to refer to sources that I have used</td><td></td><td></td></tr>
</table>

Prior learning

Think about zoos or cycling in cities. How would you describe your attitude?

I am thinking about ....

Tick (✓) one.

Strongly in favour	In favour	Neutral	Against	Strongly against

Now complete these sentences to explain your thinking.

1 I am (describe your attitude) .... to (zoos/cycling – choose one)

2 This is mainly because ....

3 In addition, ...

4 Furthermore, ...

5 Finally, ...

Starter activity

The topic I am working on today is:

....

Arun has been developing a persuasive discussion on the issue of cycling to school. Read his argument on the download that you teacher will give you.

Highlight any words/phrases that you could use when persuading someone to take action on your issue.

Main activity

Arun used a 'skeleton plan' to develop his ideas for his persuasive discussion on the issue of cycling to school. Look at his plan (your teacher will give this to you). Notice how he puts down his ideas and where he got them from.

Use the 'skeleton' planning framework below to plan a persuasive discussion text on your issue.

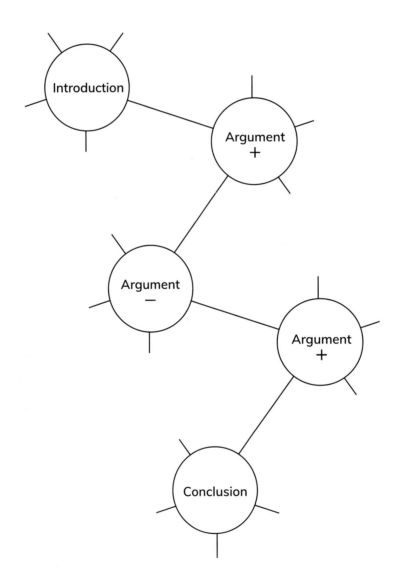

Class discussion

Different groups of people may well have different perspectives on your issue. Who will you be trying to influence? Will you have to change the arguments that you present depending on who you are talking to?

Independent reflection activity

Check your learning goals

If you are sure you have met them and can give a reason why put a '★'.

If you think you have met them put a '☺'.

If you think you are not quite there yet put a '☺'.

Developing communication skills: Lesson 4

Communication learning objectives

6.1 Communicating information

6.2 Listening and responding

Lesson learning goals		
These are the goals for this lesson. You will return to this table at the end of the lesson for the independent reflection activity.		

My learning goals To develop my knowledge and understanding about:	I think	My teacher/ partner thinks
how to tell other people about an issue so that they can understand it better		
how to listen to what someone tells me about an issue		

Prior learning

Look at your plan from Lesson 3. Use it to tell your partner the key points of what you intend to say about your issue. See if they can complete the skeleton diagram with what you say.

Listen to your partner as they tell you the key points of what they intend to say about their issue. See if you can complete the skeleton diagram with what they say.

Class discussion

How can a speaker structure what they say to make it easy for a listener to pick out the key message?

Starter activity

The topic I am working on today is:

....

Look at the notes you made in Lesson 3 about your issue. Look at the words/phrases you highlighted on Arun's introduction.

Write the introduction to your discussion.

....

....

....

....

....

Main activity

Look again at the notes you made in Lesson 3 about your issue.
Look at the words/phrases you highlighted in the rest of Arun's discussion.

1   Write the second paragraph of your discussion.

   ....

   ....

   ....

2   Write the third paragraph of your discussion.

   ....

   ....

   ....

3   Write the fourth paragraph of your discussion.

   ....

   ....

   ....

4   Write the conclusion to your discussion.

   ....

   ....

   ....

Peer feedback

Present your discussion to your partner and ask them to tell you:

1   Were you clear and did your partner understand what you want to happen?
2   Did you include facts and opinions?
3   Was there some detail which made your argument believable?

4 Did you tell them where some of your facts came from?

5 Did you organise similar points together?

6 Did you show that you had understood the other side of the argument?

Two things you did well (write what they tell you here):

⭐ ....

⭐ ....

One thing that you could do better (write what they tell you here):

 ....

Independent reflection activity

Check your learning goals

If you are sure you have met them and can give a reason why put a '★'.

If you think you have met them put a '☺'.

If you think you are not quite there yet put a '☺'.

Self-assessment Lessons 3–4

How will I know if I have achieved my learning goals?

Use this activity to reflect on how well you have progressed over the last two lessons.

Tick (✓) 'Achieved' if you are sure you have made good progress with this skill and can give an example.

Tick (✓) 'Not there yet / with help' if you need some further practice so that you can make more progress.

If you tick 'Achieved', then challenge yourself to make further progress in the next section.

If you tick 'Not there yet / with help', there will be the chance to consolidate this skill in future lessons.

Continued

Communication learning objectives To develop my knowledge and understanding about:	Not there yet / with help	Achieved	Example
communicating information			
listening and responding			

Reflect on your responses in your self-assessment and identify one area for improvement.

One area I want to improve in is:

....

How I will improve:

....

Challenge topic review

Think about the Challenge topic you have been exploring and complete the following statements.

I was surprised to discover/explore that ....

....

I did not know ....

....

I now think ....

....

5

Getting better at communication skills: Lesson 5

Communication learning objectives

6.2 Listening and responding

Prior learning

Imagine someone told you that they had a low-cost and easy-to-implement solution to the local issue you have identified as part of your Challenge topic. What questions would you ask them?

Share your ideas in a class discussion.

Starter activity

Zara has been listening carefully to Arun's discussion of the cycling to school issue. She has annotated a transcript of Arun's speech – your teacher will give you this as a download.

In your pairs, one person should take the role of Zara; the other should take the role of Arun.

1   How do you think Arun would respond to Zara's questions?
2   How do you think Zara would respond to Arun's answers?

Main activity

The topic I am working on today is:

Take turns with your partner to listen carefully to each other's discussion of their issue. If you can, annotate a transcript of your partner's speech as you listen.

1   Ask your partner questions.
2   Listen carefully to their answers.
3   If you need to, ask further questions for clarification.

Independent reflection activity

Check your learning goals

If you are sure you have met them and can give a reason why put a '★'.

If you think you have met them put a '☺'.

If you think you are not quite there yet put a '☹'.

Self-assessment Lesson 5

How will I know if I have achieved my learning goals?

Use this activity to reflect on how well you have progressed over the last lesson.

Tick (✓) 'Achieved' if you are sure you have made good progress with this skill and can give an example.

Tick (✓) 'Not there yet / with help' if you need some further practice so that you can make more progress.

If you tick 'Achieved', then challenge yourself to make further progress in the next section.

If you tick 'Not there yet / with help', there will be the chance to consolidate this skill in future lessons.

Communication learning objectives To get better at:	Not there yet / with help	Achieved	Example
communicating information			
listening and responding			

Reflect on your responses in your self-assessment and identify one area for improvement.

One area I want to improve in is:

....

How I will improve:

....

Challenge topic review

Think about the Challenge topic you have been exploring and complete the following statements.

I was surprised to discover/explore that ....

....

I did not know ....

....

I now think ....

....

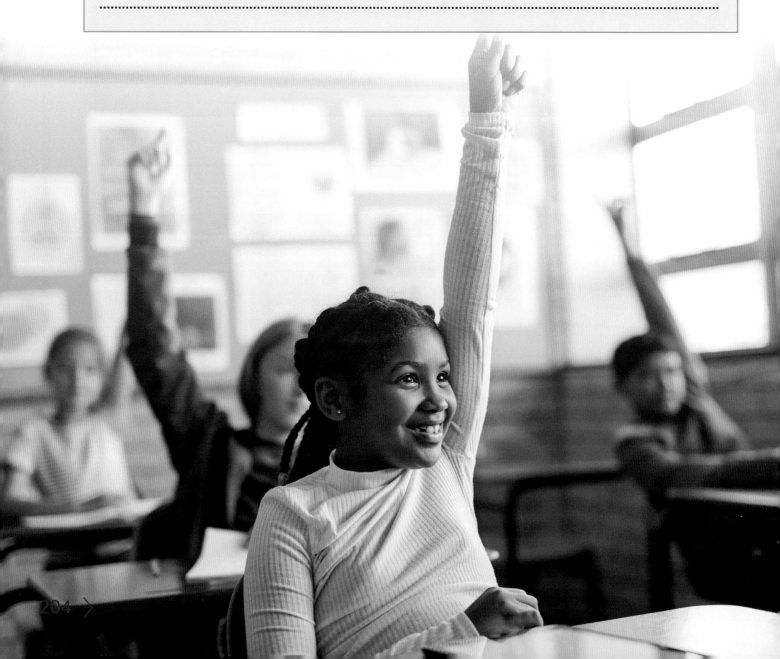

Glossary

analyse
In general, to look at something in more detail; for example, in order to understand the different parts that it consists of. In Cambridge Primary Global Perspectives, analysis may involve understanding different perspectives on a topic or issue, or how different causes and consequences are related to one another. Analysis may also involve understanding data presented as numbers or in the form of graphs, charts or tables.

annotation
Annotating a text is where the reader writes down thoughts and ideas next to a text they have just read. This could include picking out key ideas, commenting on the writer's perspective or interesting vocabulary choices.

bin
A container that is used to put waste in. 'Trash can' or 'garbage can' in US English.

cause
The reason why something happens; for example, one of the causes of global warming is the burning of fossil fuels.

collaboration
Working together with other people to achieve a shared outcome, or to resolve an issue or problem.

communication
Sending and responding to information by speaking, writing or using other media such as digital technologies. Communication also requires skills such as listening and reading so that information can be received.

consequence
The result of something; for example, global warming is the consequence of burning fossil fuels such as coal, natural gas and oil.

consolidate
To pull together and strengthen, for example, your knowledge and understanding.

evaluation
In general, deciding if something is useful for a particular purpose. In Cambridge Primary Global Perspectives, evaluation may involve deciding how useful a source of information is, or how effective an argument for or against something is, etc.

feature	The features of a source are the parts that help you to find information in the source, such as sub-headings, bullet-pointed lists, diagrams, etc. They also help you to identify the distinctive characteristics of a source, such as the headline of a newspaper article or the list of ingredients in a recipe.
global	Anything that relates to the whole world. For example, a global perspective is a way of looking at a topic that is shared by many people from different countries around the world; a global issue is one that affects people all around the world.
greenhouses gases	Gases such as carbon dioxide (CO_2) that lead to global warming.
influence	To have an effect on the ideas, development or actions of an individual or group of people.
issue	A topic that needs discussion because people have different perspectives about the best way to take action in order to resolve it.
justification	When you justify something, you give reasons for it, or explain why you have chosen it. For example, 'My justification for not eating meat is that we can produce more food for everyone if we use farmland for growing crops instead of for raising animals.'
local	Anything that relates to a particular place, such as a town or city, a district or region. For example, a local perspective is a way of looking at a topic that is shared by many people from the same place; a local issue is a problem that affects people in one particular place.
national	Anything that relates to a whole country. For example, a national perspective is a way of looking at a topic that is shared by many people from the same country; a national issue is one that affects people in one country.
personal	Anything that relates to you as an individual; for example, your own individual way of looking at a topic is your personal perspective.

perspective	A perspective is a point of view on an issue. People can have different perspectives for many reasons, including what they believe to be true or right.
prediction	Making a prediction is saying what you think will happen in the future.
recycling	Rather than throwing something away, that thing can be recycled by using the materials to make something new.
reflection	In general, thinking about or considering something in depth. In Cambridge Primary Global Perspectives, reflection may involve thinking about how well you have achieved your learning goals, how your thinking about an issue or your behaviour has changed, how much progress you have made in developing your skills, etc. You may also be expected to reflect on your personal contribution to a team effort, and on the benefits and challenges of working as a team.
research	In general, investigating an issue or topic in order to get information about it. In Cambridge Primary Global Perspectives, research may involve making questions or predictions to help you find out more about an issue, finding sources that contain useful information, carrying out investigations using interviews and/or questionnaires, and presenting the results of an investigation.
source	Anything written, spoken or visual/graphic that gives you information about a topic.
stakeholders	Stakeholders are people who have an interest in a topic. They may be for or against that topic, have some control or influence over it, or be in some way affected by it. For example, the stakeholders in the topic of air travel could include the owners and employees of airlines, the owners and employees of companies that make aircraft, people who travel by air, people who live near airports, etc.
tally	A way of counting or recording a number of items.